POST-COMPULSORY
EDUCATION II: The Way Ahead

Edmund J. King
Christine H. Moor
Jennifer A. Mundy

000000919182

SAGE Studies in Social and Educational Change
Volume 2

Ⓢ **SAGE Publications**   ·   London and Beverly Hills

For information address:

SAGE PUBLICATIONS, LTD.
St George's House/44 Hatton Garden
London EC1N 8ER

SAGE PUBLICATIONS, INC.
275 South Beverly Drive
Beverly Hills, California 90212

International Standard Book Number

0-8039-9950-X Paper

0-8039-9953-4 Cloth

Library of Congress Catalog Card No. 74-31574

FIRST PRINTING

Printed and Bound in Great Britain by Biddles Ltd., Martyr Road, Guildford

POST-COMPULSORY EDUCATION II:
The Way Ahead

The Comparative Research Unit was established at King's College, University of London, in 1970, with a grant from the Social Science Research Council to conduct a 3-year enquiry into the educational and social implications of the rapid expansion of upper-secondary education in England and four other Western European countries (France, the Federal Republic of Germany, Italy, and Sweden).

Personnel

Edmund J. King, Research Director, was concerned with the comparative study of institutional change and educational policy, and with co-ordination of the research programme.

Christine H. Moor, Research Associate, was concerned with upper-secondary students' educational and occupational ambitions, expectations, and opportunity perceptions. She also investigated the provision of counselling and careers guidance in schools, and students' attitudes towards it.

Jennifer A. Mundy, Research Associate, was concerned with curricular change and evolving arrangements for teaching and learning, with particular reference to the needs of today's upper-secondary school population.

POST-COMPULSORY EDUCATION I:
A New Analysis in Western Europe

(SAGE Publications Ltd., 1974) contains the research report in full. The present volume offers additional material, observations of a practical kind, and suggestions for policy development.

The authors published **THE DEMOCRATISATION OF SECONDARY EDUCATION** (Unesco: Series B. Opinions, No. 8) in 1971. Individually they have published several articles and conference papers on the findings of the research programme.

CONTENTS

INTRODUCTION

The Relationship of this Book to
Post-Compulsory Education I:
A New Analysis in Western Europe
and to Previous Surveys

This book is about newness in needs and prospects for the full-time education of the 16-20 age-group.

That theme is of the utmost importance today. It has in recent years attracted the attention of Ministers of Education and practitioners in the schools and colleges; but the educational and social problems which now arise from unprecedented enrolments and expectations beyond the age of compulsory schooling also arouse wide and lively interest among employers, parents, and young adults themselves.

That change in the atmosphere and tempo of discussion is by itself an indication of newness. The sense of urgency now characteristic of discussions and reform plans for this age-group has grown rapidly and insistently over the past ten years. Within less than a decade the terms in which that level of education is discussed are — in well-informed circles at least — markedly different from those used as recently as the late 1950s or early 1960s. That is not surprising when we reflect that the numbers of students enrolled full-time to the age of about 18 has doubled or trebled in as little as 15 years in several Western European countries and highly urbanised nations elsewhere. To take the case of England alone, full-time enrolments to the age of 18 totalled almost 30% of the 17-18 age-group by 1974 though the corresponding figure for the early 1950s was under 10%, and in the mid-1960s only 14%.

Nor is any marked levelling-out immediately in prospect. Even in these days of grave financial stringency, local education authorities and the Department of Education and Science recently calculated that in England and Wales some 50% of the age-group will very likely be at school or in a college at the same attainment level until the age of about 18 by the early 1980s. Adding the words 'or in a college' acknowledges one type of change which affects attitudes and teaching-learning relationships as well as curricular expectations. Already about one-third of British students enrolled full-time to the age of secondary-school completion are not in 'schools' at all, but in 'further education' establishments.

More than a quarter of the Advanced-Level certificates obtained in 1974 were prepared for in 'colleges of further education'. By themselves, those figures leave out of account two other important changes afoot at this age- and attainment-level. Vocationally linked certificates (like the Ordinary National Diplomas) customarily prepared for in further education colleges should perhaps be added to the calculation, since some of them are on the way to achieving new respectability and academic 'equivalence'. At this point no special attention is drawn to the many new kinds of separated 'secondary colleges' and 'junior colleges', or the school-'further education' hybrids now rapidly springing up, except to indicate broadly the very real newness of the institutional and curricular terms in which the education of the over-16s must be considered in our own country. These now often group together students from widely differing school experience, and with varied present interests. We have therefore to deal with a whole new range of relationships and assumptions.

All these changes in enrolment, institutional structure, expectation, course-content, resources and teaching/learning relationships in 'school' or 'college' show by themselves why up-to-date consideration of the 16-20 age-group must challenge previous provision. Then we have to think of links with learning or training prospects outside, and the vista of development ahead — perhaps with formal education or training, and certainly with personal and professional readjustment. Therefore volumes like *Post-Compulsory Education I: A New Analysis in Western Europe* (1974), and the present book with its policy-oriented conclusions from that analysis, differ substantially from previous surveys if only because the field of study is new in important ways. Different data are studied; there are new institutional adjustments and contacts; different priorities are emphasised in 'management'; and today's policy alternatives (with choices often made by different responsible bodies) have altered implications for educational instrumentation and partnership.

Newness is shown too not only in the objective field of research but also in the special orientation of the investigation which led to this and the previous volume. Different questions were asked as guidelines to the enquiry and its interpretation, and consequently in the questionnaires forming the major part of the fieldwork programme. The investigators did indeed take account of factual changes, and of contextual forces or external criteria for educational choice (and success); but they devised a novel complex of questions to focus centrally on the *educational experience of the 16-20 age-group as perceived 'from inside'*, both at present and in the perspective of young adults' development after full-time education at this level. The research tried to discover what was really happening in the schools or colleges, or what was perceived as happening by those actually engaged in the educational process in the light of students' and teachers' expectations, rather than what was officially supposed to happen.

Furthermore, within each country the survey examined full-time education in the *immediately post-compulsory period as a whole* (which no government except Sweden's has realistically done so far). Beyond formal studies, it also included more of the inner dimensions of young adults' full-time learning, training and personal development in the upper-secondary/lower-tertiary phase than have customarily been included in surveys of public education. Those neglected curricular and personal perspectives are integral to all-round understanding of young adults' education today.

The analysis was comparative, too, in its examination of questions and trends generic to this phase of education in most Western European countries, across the distinct characteristics of particular contexts or groups, and always with an awareness of critical decisions also facing young adults in similar circumstances much further afield. Problems of combining on-the-spot investigation and polyvalent analysis in this survey thus presented a new research challenge which was examined in the previous book and is the subject of a methodological note in an Appendix to this volume.

Newness also characterised the Comparative Research Unit's investigation in another respect. Previous surveys (like the International Evaluation of Educational Attainment —

IEA) concentrated almost exclusively on selected *objective* or external factors which might have an influence on *quantifiable attainment.* Among them were home background, teachers' preparation, school structure and organisation, or curricular structure within the formal 'subject' selected for survey. The central research emphasis of earlier surveys was thus on readily measurable indices of operational efficiency or 'output', in specific subject-matter or curricular elements exactly defined by the researchers and their advisers. Important *educational* dimensions beyond the formal curriculum were thus under-emphasised or even omitted. Among these were the possible effects of previous types of school experience, altered learning modes and orientation, new combinations of interest and motive in study or life-prospects. Most noticeably, questions of personal relationships and perceptions, and other subjective or qualitative aspects, were avoided. Affective, moral, and aesthetic links with the prevailing 'culture', and similar less didactic influences, were consciously excluded from nearly all earlier surveys at this level which concentrated on *scholastic efficiency.*

Post-Compulsory Education I: A New Analysis in Western Europe, by contrast, concentrated markedly on 'the inside view' from the schools and colleges, not only as a missing dimension but because this aspect is central to questions of *educational effectiveness.* It is a commonplace of educational discussion that education in any true sense takes place only when the learner identifies himself in some measure with what is learned, carries that learning forward, and initiates a process of autonomous or supported self-development likely to be viable over a long period − if not for ever. Therefore the *subjective, inter-personal, and experiential dimensions* of education strongly influenced the shaping of our enquiry and the interpretation of its results.

Though these dimensions proved difficult to measure, nevertheless nearly a million data were recorded, computed, tabulated and diagrammatically displayed from the evidence of some 12,000 questionnaires administered to as wide a range as possible of students, teachers and administrators in five countries of Western Europe. That evidence, fully recorded in *Post-Compulsory Education I: A New Analysis in Western Europe,* will be frequently referred to in the present volume, which is nevertheless intended to be a rounded statement of the main problems and issues.

The gathering of information proved valuable not simply for the factual evidence but because of the spirit in which it was solicited and offered. The research team were eager to 'get inside' the schools and colleges and to win the confidence of students, teachers, and administrators. That was necessary in order to examine the dimensions of 'newness' not only in the specific details sought but for the overall view of a *total situation as perceived generically by all those engaged in the educational process.* Evidence of the elements of newness was contributed confidentially yet positively by respondents who were made to feel themselves as partners (in some sense) in a 'participant' kind of research. This participation secured their sympathetic and co-operative contribution to an overview of educational newness affecting their contemporaries in similar situations in the countries of Western Europe, and perhaps further afield.

Information was thus examined that had not hitherto been analysed (sometimes not sought for). For example, remarkable differences were uncovered between the 'official' and the 'perceived' realities of education. The researchers refused to segregate intellectually the different kinds of institution and course or other provision for young adults over 16 (though legislation or custom does so nearly everywhere). This decision had the advantage of enabling them to survey across all the details of information from this or that course or institution what was generically common within individual countries, and often across country boundaries. At the same time it was possible to relate the immediately post-compulsory period to the longer and wider perspectives of learning, working, and living requirements for older adults — which are themselves undergoing rapid change and are already subjected to international scrutiny.

Therefore the Comparative Research Unit's investigation differed from (i) some specialist researches concerned with 'items' of curriculum or 'phases' of a system, and (ii) those international surveys which have focused on general considerations *as from outside,* or even *in abstracto.* Thus at many points the newness of the survey on which this book and its predecessor are based must be described not only in terms of new circumstances, new enrolled population (new in its dimensions and make-up), or even in the new provision or plans made to meet these new needs, but in terms of *new attitudes* which motivated the research and which contributed so much from the 'inside view' of the respondents. The implied need for new attitudes in policy-shaping and teacher-preparation for this educational level is obvious.

How then does *Post-Compulsory Education II: The Way Ahead* differ from *Post-Compulsory Education I: A New Analysis in Western Europe?* The answer is fairly straightforward. The first volume represents our fact-finding and analytical contribution; it contains the vital evidence for the practical and policy-oriented conclusions of the present volume. *This* book is addressed directly to those who have to make decisions as administrators, teachers, advisers, or simply as students seeking to familiarise themselves with the way ahead.

Our research project, sponsored by the Social Science

Research Council between 1970 and 1973, required limitation of our Report to the previously specified elements which we set out in the earlier volume. However, in preparation for that survey and in support of it, a great deal of collateral evidence was acquired. Broader insights were afforded by many respondents, by visits elsewhere, and by studies and contacts outside the purview of the original enquiry. Consequently, the present volume, though smaller, is in some ways much richer with insights likely to influence policy decisions and programming.

Beyond the questionnaire-based and interview material analysed in our earlier book, a wide range of evidence has been sifted and stored for presentation here. Some of it came from our fieldwork, or from collateral studies; but a great deal is the result of contributions from colleagues in many countries besides Britain. Our research activities brought us not only the benefits of generous co-operation in the centres where we worked or discussed our findings; they also acted as a centre of interest for many others concerned with problems of developing post-compulsory education. Thus in correspondence and conferences, as well as direct contact, much information and valuable insights have been forthcoming.

At the same time, interest in post-compulsory education (not always by that name) has been growing throughout the world. Monumental reports on particular aspects of education with a direct bearing on the post-compulsory period have also been published in the past year or two – too recently for inclusion in our first survey, but taken account of here. The feedback from our own first presentation has helped us greatly to develop some of our ideas, and to see their wider network of implications. In the present book we therefore offer as comprehensive a picture as possible of post-compulsory education's most striking features, its critical points affecting future policy, and the special implications for Britain in its Western European setting.

The chapters which follow first set out the present scene, distinguish critical factors for change, examine some expedients adopted or proposed for this level of education, and consider the signposts for the way ahead. Our final chapter draws conclusions for policy and practice in Britain and further afield — wherever the full-time education of young adults is being re-thought in all its newness.

1

THE PRESENT SCENE

Post-Compulsory Education I: A New Analysis in Western Europe presented information on 'education 16-20' as perceived by all participants — and as gathered during the 1970-1972 period in the restricted range of countries and locations brought under research scrutiny.

It will be the task of the present chapter to give a picture of collateral facts and trends contemporary with the original survey, and to present further pieces of evidence or analysis which bring the picture up to date. As always, the main emphasis is on Britain, even when we are conscious that our policy-oriented observations are more widely relevant.

Of course, events elsewhere form important parts of public awareness in whatever country is considered. In addition to general information from the mass media on new manifestations of young adults' expectations in education and life-style, it is important to know (for example) that since the publication of the research report the age of civic majority has been lowered to 18 in France (1974) and the Federal Republic of Germany (1975). Likewise, though enrolments in full-time post-compulsory education continue to grow, there has been some slackening of the pace of increase in several countries or special sectors, and in a few instances university enrolments (for example) have actually dropped. Yet at the same time more countries have passed laws enabling workers to return to formal education with pay or supporting grants; France, Italy, Sweden, West Germany, Norway and the Netherlands are recent examples. Such circumstantial evidence seems bound to influence thinking about future policy in any similar country. That is especially likely when Ministers and officials meet under the aegis of the Council of Europe, the European Economic Community, and OECD; for then the education of the 16-20 age-group is appraised in countries of similar background or with similar expectations in view.

A NEW CONTEXT FOR DISCUSSION:
A NEW URGENCY

Increasing consciousness of widely significant factors behind domestic events has been given greater urgency by the world's fuel and food crises within the 1970s alone. Within that growing community of interests the impact of events or shocks within the field of education assumes greater importance. It is impossible anywhere on the continent of Europe to go very far in any educational discussion without some consideration of 'the events of 1968'. That period marks a turning-point in educational thinking for many countries, not only with reference to university and upper-secondary students but in an extended range of repercussions. We mention those events simply as examples justifying a sense of urgency and crisis, and refer in support to the writings of Messieurs Janne and Géminard for the Council of Europe, and to the enquiries and publications of

M. G. Vincent and Mlle. M. Aumont.* Such writings strongly
reinforce our own evidence and conclusions.

The pace and scope of change in life-styles, occupations
and social relationships have made young adults beyond the
age of 16 conscious everywhere of their 'frontier' position.
The traditional uncertainty of the young person on the
threshold of adult life, found even in more settled times
which had initiation ceremonies or tutelage for new arrivals,
is aggravated immeasurably in our circumstances. Adult roles
and jobs themselves are challenged by every occupational
shift. The narrow horizons of knowledge and belief which
sufficed in former times no longer make sense enough for the
modern world. The locus and focus of authority have shifted.
New communications bring awareness of new opportunities
and expectations, perhaps with alternative norms in personal
privilege and civic obligations. To find one's footing in this
changing world perplexes even mature adults, who for one or
two generations already have learned to live with uncertainty.
The gap between them and young adults is increasingly
marked. Indeed, some observers have declared that, roughly
speaking, four or more adult categories are now distinguishable: those aged approximately 16-20; those between about
20 and 26 or 27; then at least two other categories mainly
shaped by either war-influenced or pre-war childhood.

It is worth remembering in connection with those
supposed categories that 20 is an average age for completing
secondary school or its vocational counterpart in many

*H. Janne and L. Géminard, *The Educational Needs of the 16-19
Age-Group* (Council of Europe, 1973); G. Vincent, *Le peuple lycéen*
(Gallimard, 1974); M. Aumont, *Jeunes dans un monde nouveau*
(Centurion, 1973).

continental systems, while 26 or 27 is a common university graduation age. In Britain there are fashions and magazines directly aimed at the under-20s. 'New Woman' magazines appeal specially to the age-range with which we are concerned. So there may be distinct turning-points or cultural pockets characterised (or reinforced) by activities within or around the educational system.

However that may be, evidence suggests that discontinuity between our older norms or aspirations and those now accepted by adults under the age of 20 or 25-27 causes much repudiation of parental and scholastic expectations, which are marked by different fields of awareness and concern. Repudiation may be selfish or nihilistic; but it is often associated with genuine sensitivity to new interests and commitment – perhaps (in the minds of the young) with a higher moral and social sense, despite the profanities and vulgarity often used to express it.

On the ideological plane, scholars remind us that a similar tension between world outlooks characterised the Renaissance and the Reformation period, though our upheaval is faster and further-reaching. Not merely beliefs and 'authority' are questioned, but the whole basis of human relationships. Varying lengths and types of formal education are a major cause of generic differences in outlook; and the central arena for discussions of every kind for those still in full-time education is the school or college and its daily contacts. Never before has full-time education brought so many into such a 'forcing-house' atmosphere for re-thinking so many things. Moreover, school-based reorientation is reinforced by assiduous advertising, special journals, idioms of music and dance, the holiday industries, and so forth. All these external influences would add up to what the French have long called 'the parallel school', even if no scholastic ingredient were added to systematise the possibly alienating mixture. Yet the major gap between realms of experience, and the divergence in perspectives, are undoubtedly caused or accentuated in many cases by the different worlds of formal education which older adults and younger people have experienced.

One striking feature is that many students now in upper-secondary schools and universities have parents who barely completed elementary school — even in the days when elementary school was thought by the privileged to be a third-rate affair. In those days didacticism, conformity, and career slotting characterised most teaching/learning relationships and later initiation into adult life. Demarcation into social classes, careers and income brackets was usually sharp and lifelong. Young adults now do not regard distinctions even between French people and Germans (for example) as so definite. Their clothing styles and community life, despite many continuing internal divisions between them, nevertheless mark them off from most adults, even those closest to them. Though many family bonds of affection and personal regard persist, of course, these no more imply identification of purpose and commitment than does regard for a delicate great-aunt. Time and again, evidence from student documents in the 16-20 age-group reveals a broad distinctiveness of outlook and an important distance of sympathies. Such things arise from the hidden criteria by which young and old find their identification. Our own evidence shows those criteria to be numerous and telling — not least between students and their teachers.

When differences of this kind are consciously accentuated by the young adults themselves (as in sexual relations and/or political expression) they are frequently given more categorical shape; they may be classified by slogans or hardened into some sort of 'party line'. On the continent that is particularly so. The relative protectedness of British students so far should not be assumed to be permanent. Sharp-eyed compatriots tell us that a similar hardening of attitudes is no more than a decade ahead in Britain — if that. Criticism is yearly more explicit; it is also harder to counter because older adults are less sure of themselves than they used to be. 'Father is finished', 'School is dead', 'Is God dead?' and similar phrases repeat more insistently the youthful misgivings long ago of those who are now old. Nowadays they are reinforced by youth's own press and organisations even in school, as well as by the salacious periodicals and entertainments of the older generation. All these influences add up to a quite altered context for the education of the young adult today.

International communications between young adults themselves have also developed in a crescendo. We see this most obviously in the student movements which have disturbed so much of higher education. The tide of controversy often prevalent there has swept into many secondary schools and other institutions at the same level. Though it would be a very great mistake to suppose that there is a 'common culture' of young adults across so many diverse regions, backgrounds, political views, and personal characteristics, nevertheless all the evidence shows a tendency for many differences to be submerged in common sympathies and corporate awareness of 'youth'. Such solidarity is most evident in the face of real or imagined 'oppression', or against the unsatisfactoriness of 'the system', or simply because of bewilderment occasioned by manifest 'newness' in present circumstances.

Hitherto countries generally administered their provision for the different kinds of upper-secondary education (on a much smaller scale than now, and with a restricted purview of course requirements) in separate institutions with remarkably different outcomes. More now think increasingly in terms of a common base or a 'polyvalent' educational programme for at least part of the upper-secondary provision — often with the further expectation of some kind of 'recurrent' education thereafter. Consequently a whole new set of questions is at present being asked about post-compulsory education by responsible bodies who had not previously suspected the distinct existence or the generic challenge of a new world of education for young adults.

A NEW CONCEPT: THE EDUCATION OF YOUNG ADULTS

Post-compulsory education, though restricted, has been considered by many countries for a long time to be the most important part of their secondary education systems. Many British grammar school headmasters and headmistresses never weary of repeating that the 'sixth form' (beyond 16) is the crown and justification of the entire secondary school course. What they have in mind, as a rule, is a pre-university atmosphere of greater friendship and discussion based upon more intensive specialisation in a restricted range of subjects — undertaken by a dwindling minority of the school's initial enrolment after internal selection on the way up, and after the first hurdle of public examinations about the age of 16. In other countries there is much less specialisation. There is usually no external examination at the age of 15 or 16 either, in these days; but rigorous processes of selection (by holding back pupils, by judicious choice of courses, or by channelling the 'less able' into less esteemed institutions) generally result in a similar maintenance of an academic pre-university forcing house.

That tradition dies very hard. In some countries more so

than in Britain, the university influence is felt extremely strongly at this level, because the majority of those who eventually pass the school leaving examination will have either direct or very easy access to the university and course of their choice in most instances. In a few countries like Japan, there is also a direct link between end-of-school performance and access to lifelong careers in distinguished firms or occupations after a transition stage in a distinguished university. To a greater or lesser degree, the same kind of force is felt in most upper-secondary schools of academic type everywhere. During the past two decades that pre-determining influence has been less keenly felt in some schools in Britain; but in our most distinguished establishments (socially speaking) it is still felt with hardly diminished vigour.

As everyone knows, both old-style and new-style alternatives to academic upper schools (such as comprehensive school sixth forms, or commercial institutes, and even the junior parts of technical colleges) have generally been held in lower estimation. Older people will remember that such distinctions were more marked in the past than at present; and on the continent until very recently indeed the hierarchies and class distinctions of education were more marked still. In Britain before the 1960s, the great majority of the few continuing their full-time education beyond the age of 16 did so in selective grammar school sixth forms, especially those in the private sector of so-called Public Schools. Students pursuing commercial or technical courses generally did so on a part-time basis with a very large drop-out ratio. High failure rates and austere conditions made such non-academic alternatives seem even less worthy of esteem.

Continental tradition was different in several ways; but it had the same result. As many as 40% of the young Italians continuing their education beyond the end of the 'middle school' (i.e. after the age of 14 or more) did so in technical or vocational institutions of upper-secondary level as recently as the beginning of this decade. Then they had no other outcome than a vocationally usable certificate. That was a characteristic continental situation. To take an extreme example, this kind of distinction also segregated the elementary school teachers who themselves were *trained at this level* from secondary school teachers who were *educated at the university* after completing a traditional grammar-school course which was favoured in every way — socially, pedagogically, and materially.

It is only during the immense reforms which have overtaken many school systems during the past generation that a systematic overview has begun to be taken of the post-compulsory phase with its extremely varied types of course and institution. In fact, the different types of upper-secondary establishment and course have long been administered by quite separate Ministry of Education departments if not indeed by other Ministries. No such marked cleavage was felt in Britain, though British 'schools' are to this day administered under different regulations from 'further education' conducted at exactly the same attainment- and course-level.

One great conceptual change has been the acceptance of some sort of equivalence, if not common purpose and need, across the entire range of immediately post-compulsory provision. By that is meant the recognition that hitherto despised fields of interest or career prospects might well be accommodated in a kind of expanded 'sixth form' or its foreign counterpart, leading students on to a pre-university certificate or diploma. To take but one example, the French now have 20 varieties of the formerly unique *baccalauréat*, which even in recent years had only five possible groupings of subjects for the examination. Some of the newer kinds of *baccalauréat* on the technical side definitely belong to 'applied studies'; yet they still give automatic access to higher education, which in that country is indeed the mark of respectability. The detail does not matter as much as the spirit of change.

Alternatively, continental institutions once narrowly confined to particular types of course have broadened their base of intake and teaching, claiming 'parity of esteem' at the same upper-secondary/lower-tertiary level. Such claims and counterclaims, as well as the need to accommodate *somehow* a body of volunteer students greatly exceeding our British proportion, have compelled planners and administrators to take a fresh look at upper-secondary comparability – and sometimes indeed at a possibly 'comprehensive' solution to the problems of re-accommodating education at this level. The most conspicuous example of this new tendency is Sweden, which since 1971 has made a comprehensive or multilateral upper-secondary school beyond 16 universal for the whole country after two decades of carefully observed experimentation.

Even where large-scale structural reorganisation of the type just indicated has not yet taken place, nevertheless the conceptual change in this direction is marked by readiness to re-consider the common elements (perhaps common problems) of 'educational efficiency' at this level. Existing school and college structures have been overwhelmed by ever-growing enrolments, bringing new populations and expectations to post-compulsory education – often from already reorganised lower-secondary schools. New modes of learning through modern programmes or with different career expectations are thus brought into the post-compulsory phase at its very beginning. There can be no question of responding fully to new needs within older patterns of institution and course in the majority of cases. Old instruments seldom lend themselves to new purposes; and old attitudes on the part of teachers and organisers are sometimes barely intelligible even to eager young learners, if these are unfamiliar with the entire background of expectation familiar to teachers.

Curricular reform alone (for abler students too) has challenged many norms and modes as well as familiar content; and that confrontation is all the more marked because few teachers have been prepared for the education of such large numbers in rapidly evolving school systems; they have to cope with many attainment levels and such varied expectations of any possible outcome. Therefore, the very question of an adequate teacher supply even according to older expectations becomes increasingly difficult amid so many competing claims for skilled personnel, and with the contemporary growth of higher education. These are but practical details of the problem of re-thinking post-compulsory education; but they forcefully illustrate the need for a new conceptual as well as a new organisational approach.

Nearly all countries' inherited school and college systems have been meticulously prescribed by law. Certificates, courses, teacher supply, methods of recruitment and rites of passage are likewise prescribed. In Britain we have less rigidity, though there is plenty of that in 'further education' at this level, notably in courses leading to Ordinary National Diplomas and the like. Teachers' timetables and working conditions fall into 'official' or customary hierarchies, according to their country. Problems of reorganisation are therefore severe. It is marvellous that in Britain so much re-thinking has taken place, and so much structural readjustment.

The fact remains, however, that very few local education authorities have yet recognised that for fresh thinking about 'sixth forms' and the like within their territories they are almost compelled by the present requirements of young adults' education to set up new working commissions or inter-departmental units of some kind, simply to analyse and comprehend the *generic* requirements of the over-16s. Who is really to take care of the education of the over-16s? Whose responsibility is it to see their problems as a whole? Within what parameters and perspectives is the effective use of all teaching/learning resources to be re-thought — let alone reorganised?

The British tradition of devolved partnership has left many local and sectional interests unco-ordinated even at the level of a single large local education authority. What about the country as a whole? Then who is to ensure proper preparation and concurrent support for the teachers in post-compulsory education? How are teachers who were prepared for quite different expectations (long ago, perhaps) going to be helped to serve new needs? At the upper-secondary level alone the conceptual reorientation is exacting. When we take account also of its relationship to changes in the lower part of the secondary school, and in higher and 'recurrent education', reorientation is even more demanding and crucial. What is more, it is not a case of once-and-for-all re-thinking, but of continuous re-thinking. That re-thinking cannot depend upon casual evolution, however, for which there is no time. An informed policy is essential. In present British circumstances there is plenty of opportunity for piecemeal change; but without an enlightened conspectus and a realistic perspective of development there can be no effective reform.

Perhaps the greatest single challenge arises from recent evidence about the teaching/learning and personal requirements of *young adult* students. These increasingly represent the *average* citizen, since enrolments to the age of 18 are expected to reach a proportion of over 50% by the early 1980s in Britain too. The prime task is at all costs to approach their education *afresh and generically*. There is little or no point in simply distinguishing 'traditional' from 'non-traditional' sixth formers (as the Schools Council Working Papers nearly always did). There is no point either in isolating statistics of one category of establishment from another at this level, especially if differently housed students are increasingly pursuing similar or identical courses. Moreover, the final outcome and 'effectiveness' of education or training appear to depend upon attitudes and atmosphere rather than traditional details of course specifications and objectives.

Consortia of institutions and resources in several British counties and cities already make it impossible to sustain the nice distinctions of the past. Young adults themselves increasingly migrate from one type of course or establishment to another. Besides, linear progression from one type of certificate or course to its traditional follow-up is no longer acceptable to many, or always desirable. We may postpone for the moment the question of those who might leave education altogether, and consider those intending to stay in education or to resume full-time studies after an interval.

Even for those intending to continue studies in higher education immediately, the development of degree courses based on a 'unit' or 'module' structure, and on 'fields of interest' in new 'schools' such as European Studies and Environmental Studies, brings into question the traditional straightforward flow from secondary-school subjects to university subject specialisation. 'Sandwich' courses in higher education introduce a further consideration. So does the injection of new studies at a fairly elementary level in the *post*-secondary phase, such as new languages or computer science. We always did this anyway for young parsons wanting to learn Greek and Hebrew; but we are slow to acknowledge that a similar need is becoming widespread across a more modern range of interests simply because after-school learning is changing faster than school concepts and curricula. When we add to the picture the prospect of periodic relearning, and the recognition of *profiles* of attainment (with relative ignorance in some fields flanking expertise in others), we see that categories of competence according to school-based prescriptions may have little meaning for the adult phase of learning. *The post-compulsory phase of school, indeed, should be regarded as the first phase of adult education.*

The heart of the matter is not to be found in administrative change of institutions or courses, or in the technical and social adaptation of curricula before, during and after the age-range we are thinking of. It lies in the lifelong expectation of *autonomous responsibility* for one's continued education and development beyond the adolescent stage. That presupposes careful guidance and counselling, with every other kind of support. This vivid perspective alone makes nonsense of most conventional categories of establishment, course, or expected outcome. If nothing had happened objectively to change the apparatus and orientation of our educational inheritance, that internal and subjective change of attitude in our times would mark a huge turnabout − even for students who are already new (and conscious of being new) in so many other important respects.

It would be foolish to pretend that students as a whole (or any considerable body of them and their teachers) see anything like the whole picture of transformation, especially in such a pervasive and sophisticated enterprise as education.

(In fact, surprisingly unquestioning and conventional attitudes in students alternate with vivid flashes of new vision.) Nevertheless, the perceptions and experiences drawn from the post-compulsory scene today provide cumulative clues to new questioning, and at least some provisional answers. The task is to draw those perceptions together, analytically and comparatively, so as to yield generic insights. That is what this book is all about.

With more research, still more analysis, and not least with careful co-ordination of evidence already to hand, the great debates of education can be profitably conducted afresh at this 'frontier' point. That is why so many of today's critical decisions are being thought or re-thought precisely at the post-compulsory level, which thus becomes pivotal not only for the participants but for reformers everywhere.

These remarks are qualitative, and may therefore seem less pressing than such practical problems as providing 'roofs over heads'. But even by this criterion we have an urgent responsibility to think afresh. The 16-19 population in England and Wales alone numbers over 3.25 millions. If half (or more) remain in full-time education and/or training at the upper-secondary/lower tertiary level, there is no educational home for them in existing provision. The varied qualitative aspects, and questions of possible innovation, are urgently thrust before us by the very need to provide the simplest educational necessities — such as premises, teachers, and an opportunity to study anything.

To get the situation into a developmental perspective for the next decade we may note too that in 1975 the same percentage of young Britons were in *higher education* as stayed to complete secondary education only 10 years before. We have still some way to go before reaching our neighbours' percentages.

32

2

FACTORS FOR CHANGE, AND 'CRISIS POINTS' WITHIN EDUCATION

So far we have been thinking mainly of circumstances changing around the educational system, rather than within it. Yet evidence of change everywhere does add up to a powerful argument for a *new style of education,* especially for the over-16s in their position on the edge of a life of new relationships.

No matter how apparently familiar the institutions, courses and career perspectives may seem, the certainty that most careers of the later 20th century will be altered from our present expectations seems bound to make today's teaching/learning experience different from what would have been normal two or three decades ago — for example, at the time of the Butler Act of 1944. Traditional structures, content, methods and orientation in education are challenged by the expansion of knowledge and its applications, by changes in the occupational and social hierarchy, and by international events. Perhaps the greatest challenge is within. 'The change in the composition of the sixth form is one of the continuing social changes the system has to adapt to or perish', said *The Times Educational Supplement* on 5 July 1974. Indeed, it is arguable that greater changes are still to come; the experience of other countries points in that direction.

The very special newness of the young adults' world and educational needs will not be appreciated unless that newness is seen as a response to a wider sweep of change. After all, in every generation the frontier position of young adults and the intensity of their learning experiences as they confront the world of their elders has to some extent 'made all the world seem new', even when things were stable or change was slow. But we are not now moving consecutively along a path from the past to the future; and, even if we were, the accelerated changes in everything education has to cope with would doubtless demand new handling and new relationships.

Many observers now believe that a *whole new attitude* to learning and working relationships is called for throughout society, partly because of the speed of change, partly because of the immense scatter and obsolescence of specialised knowledge, partly because of mistrust of previous assumptions of perpetual expansion, but partly also because of the need for more social cohesion through better communication and fuller partnership. Some speak of a 'communications society', now not merely feasible because of technological development but absolutely necessary because socio-political expectations demand it.

According to this view, technological and social change has moved us on from an industrialised and 'managed' or technocratic organisation of life to one which requires continuously creative response and successive judgements in an expanding proportion of society (if not all of it). Clearly, the feedback from those judgements needs to be gathered up, re-diffused, and acted upon. Therefore, the emphasis is increasingly on 'participant' learning with feedback within a 'communications society' in which to some degree all learn and all teach all the time. Historians, industrial consultants, and educators have in recent years supported this general conclusion from different standpoints.* Our own 'participant research' approach exemplified this new attitude.

THE NEED TO COMMUNICATE

It would be out of place here to develop that particular theme in any detail; but, in differing degrees of emphasis, allusions to the need to communicate recur in students' (and some teachers') responses to our questionnaires. In many of the post-1968 student recommendations soberly printed, and carefully considered by educational policy-makers, perceptions of the kind mentioned above recur by implication if not explicitly. That is but one example of the way in which the 'inside view' of those participating in 'education 16-20' mirrors the perceptions of scholarship or political expertise. That is the level of alertness we are talking about, not the manifesto-writing of party activists, since these are often repudiated or at least logically negated by the kind of subtlety we are considering.

Consequently, throughout this book we come across repeated allusions to mistrust of 'official' contrivance, of 'manpower production' in the old style of slotting units into

---

*A few references are given, which together show the relevance of these views to fresh thoughts on education: J. Galtung, 'Social Structure, Education Structure and Lifelong Education: the Case of Japan' in *OECD: Reviews of National Policies for Education* (Japan 1971), 131. E. J. King, *Other Schools and Ours* (4th edn., 1973), 66 ff. W. Boyd and E. J. King, *The History of Western Education* (10th edn., 1972), 486 ff. The Hudson Institute, *The United Kingdom in 1980* (1974). R. L. Heilbroner, *An Inquiry into the Human Prospect* (1975).

careers, and of presumptuously forecasting human development according to some blueprint. Conversely, we meet repeated allusions to the need for social response, personal experience, and collective judgement in some system of 'plastic controls with feedback'.* These are not vague socio-political aspirations; they are clearly expressed by scholars and statesmen as prerequisites for any effective education from now on.

Professor R. Hoggart has spoken of the abandonment of the Puritan work-ethic and the implications of that for education and culture. Social psychologists considering education have noted the claims of 'divergence' in education (and therefore in any selective process), instead of the compliant 'convergence' previously encouraged by the near-industrialisation of school systems and their standardising processes. More to the point now is the requirement of flexible variety which can nevertheless maintain itself in harmony with the total human enterprise that gives it full significance. No apology is offered for repetition of this theme, which constantly recurs in all educational discussions concerning young adults, for the good reason that its varied expressions add up to an argument for the educational newness which is our main concern.

The demand for, and the exercise of, devolved responsibility in modern 'management' of industry reflect this general change of attitude in society and education. Within the field of education proper, there are already

---

*The immediate reference is to Sir Karl Popper, *Of Clouds and Clocks* (1966), 16 and 21-23. A number of similar diagnoses of social and technological change in relation to educational change are discussed in E. J. King, 'Analytical Frameworks in Comparative Studies of Education', *Comparative Education,* Vol.11, No.1 (1975).

practical consequences to point to: the greater participation of teachers in curriculum development and examination procedures, like those required by Mode III of the Certificate of Secondary Education in Britain; the development of teachers' centres and 'participant' research by teachers; greater community and parental participation in school activities; a much greater sense of devolved responsibility and partnership for the students in a minority of pioneering schools. Exciting and important though these innovations are, they are really the symptoms and the promise of a new idiom of technological, social, and educational interaction.

Seen in this light, several countries' recent moves towards greater local partnership (like that of the Swedish SKK in 1975) represent much more than mere administrative decentralisation. They reflect a changing educational attitude. The supply and technical development of opportunities in education may well require more centralised provision on the material plane; but the perception and effective use of opportunity 'on the ground', and the feedback required, depend on local response. A perceptive analysis of 'participant' enterprise in curriculum development and application has recently been offered by Professor M. Skilbeck in E. Adams (ed.), *In-service Education and Teachers' Centres* (Pergamon, 1975).

From the standpoint of the present book, the vital response is to gather up these observations and apply them to the case of the young adults in our schools and colleges, who by natural inclination and the very special circumstances of their position are alert to so many critical points of educational decision. What we have already referred to as the 'great awakening of young adults', and their urgent sense of the need for a 'fresh start' in many cases about the age of 16, offer educators and society at large the opportunity to take a fresh look *with* *them* at fundamental questions of educational style and relationships. These obviously affect much education during the compulsory period of schooling too, and also much higher and 'recurrent' education.

In turn, all this implies reconsideration of style for much more 'participant management' of education inside and outside formal institutions of learning. It carries implications too for the training and re-training of teachers, for the provision of facilities for learning and self-expression in all kinds of enterprise, and for the style and structure of social life generally. Young adult students are the first to tell us so; but their perceptions are reinforced by comparative studies of educational development, not to mention the considered recommendations of OECD and other international organisations. Here we repeat a remark from our first research report: 'Of course young people lack knowledge and experience; but they are beginning to perceive knowledge and experience in ways comparable to those of their most sophisticated mentors'. Even if that were not the case, adult learning and re-thinking begins at this stage. Whatever we (together with the young adults and their teachers) decide about education at this level will be pivotal for much else across the whole range of education.

WHO DECIDES THE SHAPE OF PROVISION?

That ideal vista differs greatly from present educational reality. In most countries one or more Ministries decide nationally what the shape of the school provision must be. That means a whole hierarchy of schools from kindergarten to higher education, each with its own statutory admission and leaving requirements, its well-defined supply of teachers and other learning aids, its curriculum and sometimes its methods (at least in general terms), its financial resources and the possibilities of contact with other institutions. Where public regulation is less rigid, nevertheless custom or job requirements often define the standing and role of school or college types in ways which become sacrosanct.

Other countries seldom have private schools of such importance and prestige as those in England. Outside the British Isles most independent schools are in that category because of religion. Even private establishments are constrained by the necessity to prepare their students for public examinations and perhaps for higher education (which is usually public). In some countries, too, admission to all kinds of occupations depends upon the possession of a publicly provided or approved vocational certificate. For example, it may not be possible to manage a retail shop without one.

All these considerations account for the extremely wide spread of vocational institutions, technical and commercial qualifications, and the like. As a rule, requirements are very rigidly specified. Students often have to choose (according to their qualifications) a 'package deal' course allowing no modifications in a specified institution leading to a tightly defined diploma, if they wish to continue studies beyond compulsory schooling in order to get a good job. Generally speaking, there is far more rigidity in all such requirements than can be appreciated from English experience.

It is important to spell out these details so that the difficulties of reforming the 16-20 age-range's opportunities in education can be fully understood. Moreover, in contrast to the long familiar British tradition of part-time training, and more recently sandwich education-and-training, most other places provide full-time courses.* Some of these are

---

*i.e. 'full-time' in the continental sense of beginning very early in the

provided by the Ministry of Labour or another technological Ministry. In that case the training courses are short and extremely utilitarian. They appeal, as a rule, to poorer boys and girls or others from a disadvantaged background, such as immigrants. By contrast professional or vocational courses provided by Education Ministries have tended to become lengthier and more elaborate; admission may depend upon a particular attainment level in the secondary school.

THE PERILS OF THE SEARCH FOR 'PARITY OF ESTEEM'

In due course, many such courses and the institutions which house them have either achieved a kind of parallel respectability and some sort of 'equivalence'; or else they have become incorporated in a more 'polyvalent' or comprehensive upper-secondary school. Such incorporation does not, however, bring about 'parity of esteem' for a considerable time. The so-called 'general' and more obviously pre-university courses are usually identifiable with better premises, more theoretically qualified and better paid teachers engaged for a shorter working week, better home backgrounds, and more favoured prospects for their students.

This depressingly familiar story has, however, been subjected to several major alterations in most Western European countries in the period since the end of the 1950s. The certificates or diplomas of some vocational or technical institutions have been given more academic substance by the lengthening and broadening of courses. They have either

---

morning and finishing in the early afternoon — thus allowing indigent students to be in paid employment concurrently with their studies.

given the right of admission to higher education on their own account, or have been absorbed as a new technological or commercial variant within the previously existing school-leaving or university-admission examination. Such up-grading seems socially and occupationally desirable to many people on the ground; but it can be educationally disastrous. More material of an abstract kind, perhaps irrelevant, is packed into courses. Attention to technological realities and to the need for adaptability both personally and nationally is lessened. Previous divisions between the kinds of students continuing their education are replaced by a divorce between almost any kind of establishment and the real world outside. That, of course, includes young adult contemporaries who have left full-time education for work.

In these circumstances it has often seemed socially necessary (if not occupationally) to continue in full-time education longer and longer. That formal experience is then evaluated by university-style criteria, and leads to disdain of working experience. These are at least some of the reasons for the great swell of school and university enrolments until the beginning of the 1970s. However, since that time a falling-off in the pace of increase has been noted already, especially in countries where the enrolled percentage was very high (as in Sweden).

The schools' remoteness from reality and the end-on inevitability of transfer to yet another course entailing protracted juvenile status has been increasingly repudiated by many students − not least, by the most intelligent and by those from favoured homes. Sheer boredom and frustration combined with a suspicion that 'it would not pay after all' have brought many of youth's uncertainties to journalistic prominence. Indeed there has been some graduate unemployment in many countries, or at least difficulty in getting the jobs that graduates have traditionally aspired to. Moreover, pay differentials between university graduates and those trained or qualified in other ways have been diminished almost everywhere.* In addition to doubts about long-term prospects these uncertainties have aggravated doubts about the validity of whatever educational training was undergone.

Students who have long been physically, socially, and sexually adult have been further frustrated in many places by advantages apparently enjoyed by contemporaries who have left full-time education to enter paid employment. Would-be students also have to consider grave questions of severe expense and meagre living during the long period ahead of living on inadequate grants, or of later repayment of the loans which in most countries take the place of our own students' grants. Yet the tradition and expectation of going on to higher education are so strong that most students feel trapped, especially on the European continent.

TO GO, OR NOT TO GO, TO HIGHER EDUCATION?

Let us now look more closely at enrolment figures for higher education. In October 1973 the United Kingdom's

---

*Professor G. Williams of Lancaster University concluded at the end of 1974 that the differential between those who leave before entering the sixth form in Britain and those who graduate from university had dropped during the previous six years from 15% to 7% on a lifetime's *average* earnings. This calculation probably leaves out of account, too, the earlier promotion prospects and other advantages in early employment for a bright and enterprising person. In some other countries — e.g. in Sweden — the promotion advantage of early experience of employment offering in-service training is beginning to be clearer.

universities enrolled 244,485 full-time students, of whom 46,156 were postgraduates. For international comparisons we need to add over 90,000 full-time advanced students in polytechnics and the higher courses of 'further education' colleges, with perhaps 48,000 or so at the Open University. Nevertheless that all-round total of roughly 383,000 higher education students is less daunting to administrators than some of our neighbours' figures, even if we also count in all of the 127,600 in colleges of education.

With much the same basic population as Britain's, the French had 572,000 enrolled in the first two cycles of higher education (the first four years), and 81,000 graduates enrolled for doctoral studies. Moreover, last year's *baccalauréat* figures gave an increase of about 6,500 in those entitled to begin a university course. Likewise, the Federal Republic of Germany had more than 650,000 enrolments in higher education in 1972 (18 per cent of the 19-22 age-group), with expectations of 715,000 in 1976 on the basis of *Gymnasium* enrolments at present. Italian university enrolments increased from 261,358 in 1965 to 474,727 in 1970 — and from that to approximately 900,000 last year. That meant a doubling since 1970. However, new enrolments in higher education have been dropping absolutely in Sweden (from 26,000 in 1970 to approximately 23,000 in 1972-1973).

Let us relate these figures to upper-secondary level enrolments. In Britain enrolments to the age of 18 in full-time education totalled 28.7% of the age-group in 1973 — as against a French 46% and a Swedish 82%. That suggests we have some way to go before we level out or stop increasing. The proportion of 17-18 year olds leaving all *schools* with one or more A-Levels rose from 8.9% in 1961-1962 to 15.6% in 1971-1972 — a total of 108,810; while the proportion with two or more A-Levels rose from

7.1% to 12.2% in the 1961-1971 period. A DES estimate of 1970 foresaw that 23% of the age-group would have minimum university entry qualifications by the early 1980s.

The number of students in *further education colleges* preparing for A-Levels has more than trebled since 1961. Then 10% of A-Level successes were in colleges; now those successes are more than a quarter of a greatly increased A-Level total. We recall that more than one-third of full-time enrolments at age 17-18 in Britain are now in *further education* establishments, and the proportion is growing. In addition, several local education authorities transfer all or an increasing number of the over-16s to 'further education' or hybrid colleges, whose success rate on the threshold of old-style or new types of higher education is impressive.

Figures like these, both in Britain and abroad, seemed for more than a decade to point to the inevitability of a huge increase in higher education enrolments. After all, that had already happened in the USA and Japan, where present percentages of 50% and more in post-secondary education (and the expectation of 75% in the next decade) made many observers speak of the transition from selective to 'mass' higher education – if not from 'mass' to universal higher education. Leaving out of question for the moment the quality of what is called 'higher education', the material problems of coping with huge enrolments have exercised administrators. They have given rise to such colossal enquiries as those undertaken by the Carnegie Commission in the USA, and to hundreds of publications.

On the other hand, dropout problems and simple refusal to go any further (itself referred to as 'dropping out' from the obvious expectation in many documents) have in recent years caused anxiety in many quarters – among parents and teachers, as well as among manpower planners. So as to help our analysis of what may be wrong or improvable in the early post-compulsory years after 16, it will be worthwhile to look closely at this reluctance to go on to higher education, either immediately or at any later time.

CHANGES IN EXPECTATIONS FROM HIGHER EDUCATION

What expectations lie behind the apparently slackening demand for places in universities, polytechnics and other institutions of higher education? Some falling-off in the pace of increase — increase once thought likely to continue indefinitely — has already been discussed in relation to changes in students' long term prospects. Change can be immediately economic too, since (most obviously in Britain) student life has become markedly less attractive. There has been a decline in the real value of student grants; lodgings have become more expensive and less satisfactory; the aura of 'exclusiveness' and privilege has faded; but perhaps most of all the career prospect and styles of living associated with it have been transformed.

In addition to any dissatisfaction with school or with juvenile status, therefore, potential students who are already often hankering for a 'fresh start' weigh up the 'costs and benefits' of a student career with some dismay at the uncertainties in and beyond higher education. This hesitation has repercussions right through the post-compulsory period, since it affects not simply the question of 'staying on' but the choice of studies in relation to their career implications.

These remarks apply to many countries in a similar situation to Britain's, and therefore it is a mistake to consider that our present uncertainties can be resolved on their own. Yet a few characteristics are well illustrated by British evidence. A report published early in 1972 by the

Department of Employment, *Employment Prospects for the Highly Qualified* (Department of Employment Manpower Paper No. 8, HMSO) indicated that by the 1980s more graduates would have to look for jobs in areas not traditionally associated with them, such as nursing and secretarial work. By 1980, the report estimated, the proportion of the working population with degrees would have doubled from 3 per cent in 1966 to 6 per cent (about 1,400,000). Rapid growth in the numbers of highly qualified young people was not being matched by jobs in business and the professions that were traditionally open to graduates.

The early 1970s have indeed proved difficult years for graduates seeking jobs. In 1971, for instance, jobs offered by industrial and commercial employers visiting universities were cut back by about 3 or 4 thousand. The full significance of this becomes apparent when one considers that only about four out of every ten graduates go directly into employment, and of these about two thirds have, in the past, gone into industry and commerce. So a cutback may represent a small percentage of all graduates, but a sizeable proportion of those looking for jobs.

The situation has been complicated in recent years by the growing number of unemployed *post-graduate* students competing for what would previously have been regarded as graduate level jobs. The repercussions have been felt in many sectors of employment, especially those previously spurned by graduates. A report in *The Times Educational Supplement* in February 1972 lucidly summarised the position at the time:

> The Inland Revenue and local government, which used to have to beg for graduates, are now swamped with applications . . . The Civil Service has long given up thinking of the administrative grade as the only possibility for graduates, and the executive grade has been receiving a much larger number of applications.

In the same year the Confederation of British Industry stated that there was a 'natural limit' to the number of people required by any organisation to do the type of work usually done by graduates — a limit that had already been reached by many of the larger companies which in previous years had been among the most important recruiters of graduates. The statement went on to point out that if more graduates were to be absorbed the range of job opportunities for many graduates would inevitably broaden, with the result that an increasing number would have to accept employment below the traditional level.

Yet by late 1974 the picture already looked different. A careers conference held in November 1974 was told that thousands of job opportunities were available to graduates, but were not being taken up. It seemed that the cut-backs in employers' recruitment schemes, expected in view of the current economic crisis, had not materialised, with the result that there were many hundreds of unfilled vacancies for graduates. But a problem arose from the fact that some students did not know how to 'sell' themselves, and displayed limited competence in applying for jobs. When employment conditions and prospects change so rapidly, it is obviously difficult for students and their advisers to keep abreast of new developments, yet at the same time even more necessary for them to do so. Otherwise students are basing their plans and choices, and counselling and guidance staff their advice and information, on conditions that no longer apply. Once again we have evidence of a strong case for providing much-needed accurate and up-to-date information and advice concerning opportunities for school and college leavers. A fluid, rapidly changing employment situation makes the achievement of this all the more difficult, but the need for it greater than ever before.

AN INTERVAL BETWEEN SCHOOL AND HIGHER EDUCATION?

Objective factors in the job situation certainly affect students hesitating on the threshold of higher education. In our sample, 77% of English students felt that prospects would be 'much better' after their upper-secondary education; but only 63% thought that would be so after further studies. Yet to see everything in terms of distant bread-and-butter calculations deflects attention from other misgivings about going on to higher education — *especially if this follows immediately after upper-secondary studies.* In each of the five countries we examined, some students expressed a strong desire to 'have a year off' before embarking on higher education or employment.

Similar findings are presented in K. Fogelman's study *Leaving the Sixth Form* (National Foundation for Educational Research, 1972). The school leavers who took part in his research opted heavily for a gap between school and higher education, on the grounds that it would have a 'maturing and broadening' effect. A large group felt that a year at work had (or would have) helped them to see the relevance and purpose of their studies, and also to decide whether the career to which those studies would lead was right for them. (University rectors and vice-chancellors now often agree with them.)

Further evidence comes from the Schools Council *Sixth Form Survey* (1970). Volume III of that study, entitled *Sixth Form Leavers*, shows the degree of support for a break of at least six months between school and university or college: 83 per cent of those who had had such a break were in favour of one, as were 37 per cent of those who had not.

Such findings would no doubt gladden the heart of those who suggest that university admissions should possibly be confined to students who have spent at least one year away from school. This, it is argued, would enable applicants to become aware of the alternatives, and so possibly help to reduce the inflow of students who had applied to enter university as a purely automatic next step after upper-secondary school or college.

Such ideas, long advocated by some responsible Ministers as well as employers and researchers, would doubtless find agreement amongst many people concerned with and for upper-secondary and tertiary education. But they raise a number of questions. Not least among these is how the gap between school and university or college would be filled. By a job? If so, would employers be willing and able to take on temporary workers of this sort? And would the resulting increased competition for jobs adversely affect in any way the chances of leavers whose entry into employment was to be of a more permanent nature? And if the answer is not employment, then what? Unemployment? Voluntary work, either overseas or in the local community? And what kind of financial support should young people receive during this period?

These questions could be resolved, and certainly the principle of a gap between school and higher education has much to commend it. It does seem likely that such a gap will become increasingly popular, allowing young people a breathing space to think about the complexities of educational and occupational choices. Indeed an interval between upper-secondary education and further studies or a long-term career option may become the norm in future, since other countries of every political complexion have not merely discussed the possibility but taken steps to establish the practice.

Doubts about the value of higher education have been reflected in a fall in the number of school leavers starting degree courses. According to Government statistics released in June 1974, (*Statistics of Education. School Leavers, CSE and GCE, 1972*, Vol. 2, HMSO 1974) nine hundred fewer school leavers started degree courses in 1971-1972 than in 1970-1971, even though there were 30,000 more leavers than in the previous year. The statistics, based on a 10 per cent sample of school leavers showed that 43,100 sixth formers embarked on degree courses in England and Wales in 1971-1972. The corresponding figure for the previous year was 44,000. But the drop in University entry was small: 37,350 in 1971-1972 — 160 less than a year earlier. It is worth noting that the year under survey was a period when unemployment was at a peak of more than one million. The Government statistics show that the number entering employment straight from school rose by nearly 20,000 to 443,000.

Furthermore, 1974 saw a marked drop in the number of graduates applying to train as teachers. According to statistics published in May 1974 (by *The Times Higher Education Supplement*, 31 May 1974), applications at the end of February 1974 were down by 18.5% compared with the previous year. The biggest casualty was science courses, where applications dropped by 27.3%. And the declining popularity of teaching as a career seemed to be more marked among men than women: the fall in applications from men to train as science teachers was 34.4%.

Two factors must be borne in mind here. Firstly, that later applications might to some extent reverse this trend. Secondly, one explanation for the apparently declining appeal of teaching as a career might be found in the recent wave of publicity concerning teachers' falling standard of living. In the past 35 years, the average teacher's salary in this country has declined by around 50 per cent compared with the average working wage. According to recently published statistics, 'The average wage of Britain's 475,000 teachers is £2600. The average manual worker gets £2460; the average non-manual worker receives £3020'. (*The Times: Europa*, 3 December 1974). Industrial action and demonstrations by teachers in protest against this situation have led to a lowering of their status among the public. That in its turn affects the appeal of academic careers, and the weight of advice which teachers give.

THE POPULARITY OF STUDIES

Professor G. M. Carstairs in his Reith Lectures pointed out that in the lean times of his youth students did not question the relevance of secondary school and higher studies. Their real relevance was in making possible a breakthrough into another world — professional employment and a better way of life. Those with many students from low-income countries will recognise that the same phenomenon has not disappeared. Indeed, it may be recognisable still in the socially disadvantaged sectors of any country, no matter how highly developed.

Nonetheless, even in lean times, students very often develop a genuine enthusiasm for some of their studies. The great amount of choice available in Britain and the USA facilitates this, though it does not necessarily ensure it. One important influence in liking a school or college subject is, of course, self-identification with it; to that end, its life-linked relevance may be paramount. That returns us to the subjective interest and personal commitment with which this chapter began. At the same time, such insights and enthusiasms are fostered by a skilful or admired teacher. In the romantic picture of the 'sixth form that was', some of us look back with affection to a particular teacher or a friendly working relationship with teachers and contemporaries. In these circumstances students can learn to enjoy the ardours of intellectual struggle, as one may enjoy strenuous physical exercise.

Those are not typically today's circumstances. The turnover of teachers in Inner London, for all subjects, is 28% per annum. In science subjects it is stated to be 'much greater'. Even in favoured suburbs the annual turnover is about 24%, partly because of the cost of housing and other economic comparisons. In such conditions, in some inner city areas in Britain, about half of those teaching mathematics, the sciences, and a few other subjects (some on the arts side) are not fully qualified to do so. That is more true of girls' than of boys' schools, of less privileged schools, and above al' of the over-16 level.

Today's actualities within the formal school system, especially when contrasted with real or supposed opportunities of self-advancement elsewhere, can therefore put a brake on enthusiasm. Despite the greatest of dedication and enthusiasm on the part of teachers and many students, contrasts with the 'outside world' may be disturbing. In the circumstances it is not surprising that there is evidence of a 'flight from difficult subjects' (e.g., as reported by D. Duckworth and N. Entwistle in *Educational Research,* November 1974). At first sight that looks like a choice of the arts and social sciences as against mathematics and the sciences; but a closer look shows that 'austere' academic subjects like modern languages are also neglected.

Does that reflect a shortage of well qualified and inspiring teachers, or aridly remote examination syllabuses? Does it reflect poor performance by the teachers, or by students themselves lower down the school? Does it mean a move to more 'discussable' studies of personal and social appeal? It can hardly be a response to job prospects, for these are enhanced by demanding subjects like mathematics. May we be seeing the influence of an increasing enrolment of girls? Does it simply reflect tedium with 'subjects' of any sort if they are boxed according to available texts and old-fashioned modes of examining?

Is there disaffection for the universities which seem to be the inevitable outcome of many such studies? Is there plain ignorance of what may now be studied or trained for? Certainly, new combined fields of interest in the universities themselves (like European Studies, Environmental Studies, etc.), or a more obvious career relevance, might develop popularity – if suitable teachers were available, prepared in outlook and training for new kinds of presentation and above all for the young adult learners of today.

The right sort of response to the new relationships necessary is seen in the Inner London Education Authority's adaptation of what are called 'Open University' methods to bring educational opportunities to teacher-starved sixth forms. More important than any specific innovation is the ILEAs example of students' self-reliance (guided, of course, and with much supplementary material) for roughly three-quarters of their time, some of it at a science centre outside where there is a special tutor. All innovations of this kind, however, raise important questions of continuous and collateral support services. Are there suitable texts, manuals, audio-visual materials, and supporting services around our schools and colleges – especially in areas less well endowed and less enterprising than the Inner London Education Authority? And is there effective advice or guidance for teachers and students alike? Answers to such questions can be satisfactory only if the problems of post-compulsory education are tackled on a nation-wide scale, and far beyond the usual parameters of 'school'.

These considerations show how vital it is to see school

phenomena in their life-relatedness — not in old relationships, but in their present field of force. We have to know more about those relationships as seen in school and college by the young adults themselves, even fictitiously. Still more, the whole interplay between upper-secondary, lower-tertiary, and teachers' education must be seen together.

Nor can we be satisfied with the view from one country. Japanese students are very keen to do well in mathematics because of higher education and career criteria. (As the IEA survey showed, they are also very successful.) Mathematics and physics are the 'key' subjects for the future elite in France too. We have significant variables to take account of here, including the enrolment of more students from a wider range of home backgrounds and differently organised school experience, and the influence of career expectation.

All this raises another question: whether it is *necessarily* beneficial both to young people and to society to increase full-time upper-secondary enrolments to the age of about 18 (or even to the average of about 20 in some continental countries). Planners and politicians must scrutinise the wisdom of increasing upper-secondary enrolments, at least in a school-like atmosphere, though most of them have planned for such increase until the early 1980s. Sweden, for example, has since 1971 provided opportunities of 'comprehensive' or multilateral type for 95% of the age-group to about 19. At one time Swedish schools actually enrolled about 85% (though the number has fallen off somewhat, and one-fifth of those enrolled are really 'returners' who have had work experience).

However, since 1973 there has been growing doubt about the wisdom of relying on nearly inevitable growth according to students' spontaneous choice, and also of accepting the kinds of educational content and orientation which have seemed most desirable until very recently. The emphasis, in other words, has moved from questions of accommodation and present feasibility to questions of long-term aims or desiderata. The much-quoted U68 Report on *Higher Education* in Sweden and subsequent publications have shown how concerned experts have become about the whole style and orientation of upper-secondary and lower-tertiary education, together with its articulation with whatever precedes or follows this stage. In this uncertain world, what counsel or guidance can students expect?

CHANGING ATTITUDES TOWARDS COUNSELLING AND GUIDANCE

In this section, we concentrate on the viewpoint of the *receivers* — in other words, the students in schools and colleges for whom counselling and guidance services are intended. To put it bluntly, the customers are dissatisfied! But having said that, let us look in more detail at students' views and the extent to which their needs and demands are being met.

Our own research revealed that many upper-secondary students were highly critical of the counselling and guidance services available to them, especially those dealing with employment matters. Both the quality and the quantity of information and advice came under attack, as the following tables show.

Table 1: English Students' Assessment of Counselling and Guidance Services: Amount of Help Received*

Amount of help received	about employment (% of students)	about education (% of students)
A lot	19	36
Some	41	43
Hardly any	27	15
None at all	12	6

Table 2: English Students' Assessment of Counselling and Guidance Services: Value of Information and Advice Received

How helpful	about employment (% of students)*	about education (% of students)
Very helpful	15	27
Fairly helpful	36	45
Not really helpful	10	16
Not at all helpful	9	6

*Note: The low percentage total occurs because many students who had received little or no help did not answer this question.

Table 3: English Students' Assessment of Counselling and Guidance Services: Amount of Help Desired

Amount desired:	% of Students:
Much more than at present	50
A little more	31
About the same amount	18
A little less	0.5
Much less	0.1

*Tables 1-3 are adapted from Tables 45-47 in *Post-Compulsory Education I: A New Analysis in Western Europe* (1974), pages 348-9. The whole of Chapter 18 contains much supplementary information.

These figures tell their own story. Other research has unearthed similar dissatisfaction with counselling and guidance facilities. K. Fogelman's work revealed that students who were not aiming to go to university or a college of education felt that they were particularly badly served – a frequent complaint. Even university applicants thought that the information and advice that they had received left a lot to be desired. A misleading picture was painted of the nature and content of university courses, and insufficient guidance given about the choice of A-Level subjects. Fogelman's students felt that inadequate counselling and guidance provision resulted from schools' lack of knowledge, which led to wasted time and missed opportunities.

> Even those who were evidently content with their choice of course or career commented that this was the result of good luck rather than good guidance.

A similar point was made in a report published by the Advisory Centre for Education in 1972.* The report claimed that many pupils were being allowed to fall into a trap of wasted ability by choosing the wrong A-Level subjects or applying for university courses for which they were not qualified. The blame lay with '. . . bad or unrealistic guidance at school, and insufficient independence by the students themselves. Many schools lack adequate careers guidance although university entrance is traditionally thought to be the best advised area. *The options and complications increase, but not the guidance*' (the present authors' underlining).

Much of the criticism contained in the preceding pages

Choosing a University: ʲA Guide for Applicants (ACE, 1972).

concerns advice and guidance on higher education. But how much greater is the problem for *post-compulsory students whose aspirations lie elsewhere— in 'new' or 'non-traditional' areas?* The information and advice that they receive is likely to be even *less* adequate, because the staff concerned will in many cases have no knowledge or experience of anything other than their own field and the studies which preceded it. The students are well aware of this, as one or two of their comments show.

One student who took part in our research asked for, 'First hand information as if from the horse's mouth.... Sometimes teachers don't even know what the job entails; they only learn from books, and I am sure I'm not going to take a job on their advice'. Another commented, '... teachers' knowledge is so very limited in specific fields of careers'. A third student, who felt that more emphasis should be placed on 'informal assessment of capabilities and aptitudes for certain ... types of work', remarked that, '... staff do not seem to have sufficient experience to give this kind of advice ...'.

In short, the 'new' population in upper-secondary schools and colleges means that existing counselling and guidance services *must* be re-vamped. There is clearly an overwhelming need for accurate, wide-ranging, up-to-date information and advice which reflects students' broader-based aspirations, interests and attainments. That is especially true in the case of employment, which has been — and is still — often neglected on the ground that the vast majority of post-compulsory students are destined for traditional forms of higher education or employment involving training.

No longer can counselling and guidance consist of distributing UCCA handbooks to potential university entrants, and literature about opportunities in colleges of education or traditional sectors of post-secondary employment such as nursing, banking, the Civil Service and the Armed Forces to 'the rest'. Many 'new' post-compulsory students possess neither the inclination nor the level of attainment required to enter these careers successfully, if at all. What does the job prospect really hold out to such students, who seem likely to leave without a respected credential for further study or training, and who have not been trained for anything in the post-compulsory years?

Despite vigorous assertions to the contrary by enthusiastic teachers, young people who complete post-compulsory education without formal qualifications are often at a serious disadvantage when they compete with young school leavers for available jobs. Some employers (as our research showed) prefer to recruit younger leavers and put them through their own training programmes for one or two years, rather than employ older applicants who have spent the same time in school or college.

That brings us back to the crisis of knowledge. Teachers who have counselling responsibilities need to be *au fait* with the present employment structure, its needs, and current trends — especially in new or expanding fields.

The *Times Educational Supplement's* 16+ Inquiry (1974) found that almost two thirds (64%) of school and sixth form college students felt that their school or college should do more to 'include guidance on running a home, doing repairs and bringing up children'. An equal proportion thought that more should be done to 'teach things that would be of direct use when people start work'. An even higher percentage — three quarters of the 1,250 pupils who took part in the Inquiry — felt that their school or college should do more to 'teach pupils about things like income tax, rates and insurance'.

These young people are clearly very much oriented towards the adult world of work and family life. How then do they regard the rather different world of sixth form, sixth form unit or sixth form college in which the majority experience upper-secondary education? To some extent their negative vote is shown by the migration to further education. One feature of the expansion in post-compulsory education has been what *The Times Educational Supplement* described as 'the tramp of feet from school to 'tech' '.

One standard explanation is that students in technical colleges have more freedom and adult status than their counterparts in schools or even sixth form colleges. This may be true, despite the fact that many sixth form units and colleges have few (if any) restrictions on dress, general appearance and behaviour, and have a relaxed, informal atmosphere. Only rarely — and this may be the crux of the matter — do they have a truly adult one.

Yet — as we saw earlier — upper-secondary students are not yet 'truly adult', though some of them clearly aspire to be. This situation calls for highly sensitive, perceptive and sympathetic teachers. At this point it is worth noting that *The Times Educational Supplement's* '16+ Inquiry' revealed strong demands from sixth formers for young teachers straight from university. Not yet 'contaminated by the system', they would be close enough in age, attitudes and interests to be able to understand their pupils — or so the latter thought. They might also have fuller awareness of the realities of a working life, and more up-to-date attitudes to it. At least, either because of working experience they might have had as students, or because they are more attuned to the consequences of technological change, they could be expected to recognise the need for continuously fresh thinking.

KEEPING OPTIONS OPEN AS LONG AS POSSIBLE

The employment sector is one where changes have been particularly rapid and sweeping. The resulting situation faced by today's school or college leaver has been neatly summed up in Schools Council Working Paper 40, *Career Education in the 1970s* (1972):

> It is no longer possible to contemplate a relatively stable employment world within which a pupil can find a place that will provide him with a living for half a century . . . . It follows from this that *the most-needed qualities of today's school leavers are adaptability and flexibility, together with basic skills that will enable them to undertake new and successful learning throughout their lives* (the present authors' italics).

Such adaptability and flexibility are called for at all levels of employment, for even seemingly familiar and relatively uncomplicated jobs are taking on new dimensions. For instance, junior office staff have to grapple with the complexities of reprographic and audio-typing equipment, while accounts clerks contend with computerised pay-rolls and ordering systems. At the other end of the scale – as we have seen – job opportunities for graduates and post-graduates can fluctuate rapidly and sometimes dramatically, and a person's degree often has very little visible connection with the job he or she takes after leaving university or college.

All this means that we *must* be adaptable and flexible, both in our attitude of mind and in our concepts of education and training. In terms of counselling and guidance it means that students should be provided with the range of information and advice that will enable them to take full account of all relevant factors when deciding on options. *Internal* factors include one's own interests, abilities and attainments; *external* factors encompass job or course requirements, prospects, characteristics and rewards, the state of the labour market, and so on.

Clearly, even the most flexible and adaptable upper-secondary provision cannot totally compensate for a too-rigid system earlier on in the education process. For instance, the system of early specialisation, whereby pupils have to make choices about GCE O- and A-Level work at an early stage, is frequently criticised. Very often it results in students discovering too late that they do not possess the qualifications needed for their particular choice of job or course. 'The timetable' is no excuse for prematurely forcing people into rigid channels.

To sum up, then: flexibility seems to be the keyword as far as post-compulsory education is concerned, especially in relation to careers — hence the concept of 'provisional education' referred to earlier. 'Adapt or perish' would appear to be the motto for the 1970s.

EXAMINATIONS, CREDENTIALS, AND 'RITES OF PASSAGE'

It perhaps seems unreasonable to pay no serious attention at this point to the question of examination reform at the level of British sixth forms, for that could very profoundly affect the internal relationships of every school or college. There are several good reasons, however. The first is the most obvious and most important. Schools and curricula do not exist to lead to examinations, though anyone might be forgiven for thinking so.

Two other quite practical reasons justify that omission. In the present chapter we are concerned with 'crisis points' within educational practice and experience, and are considering only indicators for a new style of educational relationship. Such things as reform proposals and experiments come later. The second main reason for leaving examination problems aside is that in our final chapter of recommendations we shall consider transitional proposals for curricular reform in post-compulsory education in relation to the possibilities of examination reform. Yet, as long as we are not trapped into profitless detail which may soon be out of date, we ought to consider a few key questions. For example, need there be examinations at 16-plus? And if so, what relationship should those have to examinations two or three years later?

British schools stand almost alone in having significant 'academic' examinations (General Certificate of Education, Ordinary Level – or GCE O-Level) about the age of 16 in already selective schools. The examination can, of course, be taken in any kind of school; but it originated in the selective grammar schools. Other countries' systems often have a completion examination at the end of compulsory school; but that is not as competitive as the British Certificate of Secondary Education (CSE) with its grades and comparisons with the GCE, though it is clearly intended to give a permanent appraisal of the compulsory period of studies. Leading educational advisors in Britain now feel either that there should be no public examination at 16 or that, if there is, it should not be so strongly influenced by the GCE example, with marked effects upon the teaching and learning which lead to it. Primacy is increasingly given by such advisors to curriculum considerations, rather than to the examinations as rites of passage or as job credentials; and it is in that perspective that we say a few words about them here.

Between the ages of 16 and 18 or so, there has been a blizzard of new examination proposals in Britain during the last 10 or 20 years. The most notable of these are contained in the three Schools Council Working Papers 45, 46 and 47 (Evans-Methuen Educational, published in 1972 and 1973). These deal respectively with the material indicated in their titles: *16-19: Growth and Response, I. Curricular Bases; 16-19: Growth and Response, II. Examination Structure;* and *Preparation for Degree Courses.**

Obviously these books contain many valuable insights and helpful recommendations on the broader issues of education at this age range; but as contrasted with other recent studies, those Working Papers concentrate to an astonishing degree on English assumptions as circumscribed by a traditional or slightly modified framework of examinations. Radical alternatives such as the substitution of completely different forms of assessment, or the abolition of momentous public examinations before the age of about 18, lay outside the Working Parties' terms of reference and were therefore left unconsidered. Paradoxically, indecision left the possibility of *three* examinations being in force, at 16, 17, and 18.

For many years it has been clear that the traditional school-leaving examination at A-Level (though largely devised by schoolmasters under a university aegis) has set parameters for curricular development at the upper end of secondary schools. This curriculum has borne less and less relation to most students' needs, and even to university requirements. The Vice-Chancellors and College Principals in Britain and their counterparts on the continent of Europe, as well as the Association of University Teachers and unions of teachers in secondary schools and technical colleges, have all criticised secondary school curricular rigidities and over-specialisation and have proposed more broadening and flexibility. Such criticism has been applied even to studies intended to lead to

*Collectively known as the Briault-Butler proposals.

higher education. It has even greater force in the case of less advanced students or those not intending or needing to specialise.

It was primarily for these latter groups that a new Certificate of Extended Education (CEE) was proposed by the Schools Council, either to replace A-Level or in some measure to merge with the latter. Likewise, the Certificate of Secondary Education (CSE) had already made very considerable strides as an alternative to the traditional O-Level. Special attention should be given to Mode III in the CSE (now being extended to other examinations), which relies heavily on teacher participation in the planning of curricula and in the examination procedures themselves.

An outline of the progress of examinations and their reform is presented in our earlier book (pages 128 ff.). Here it is enough to say that one broad conclusion is now generally accepted: that studies in the upper-secondary level in Britain are much too restricted in number and range, and in any examination at the age of 18 not less than five well-spread fields of study should be included. How and by whom the assessment should be made raises important questions, e.g., about the already overwhelming advantage which some distinguished or socially favoured schools have in securing higher education admission for their students. Reliance on internal examinations (as in Germany) enhances the criteria applied by 'prestigious' schools. External and neutral examiners doubtless look for objective merit by nationally or socially relevant criteria, and might well reward initiative not previously encouraged either by traditional schools or by familiar examinations.

Our own survey shows plainly that in all countries the pursuit of a good job or of access to promising courses of further education and training is a main incentive for the majority of students in post-compulsory education. There is nothing surprising about that. If we had gone further afield to really poor countries like India or almost any African territory, an almost fanatical zest for study would be directly linked with the vocational objective. Evidence from the poorer parts of England and Wales emphasises the importance of vocational ambition not only in motivation but in the choice of subjects. Against this background it would be unworldly to underestimate the importance of the search for credentials.

Obviously credentials are necessary to guarantee the competence of students (as of doctors or lawyers); but they should indicate present capability as well as attainment, and be reliable indicators for future performance. Yet existing school examinations (including those familiar in Britain) have long been shown to be very imperfect predictors of university attainment or behaviour. Consequently, Scholastic Aptitude Tests bearing little (or less) relation to the content of the curriculum studied, or to the varied chances of a student's school experience, have been developed in the United States and here as alternatives or supplements to familiar school-leaving examinations. Such a move leaves schools and students more freedom to concentrate on the desirable things in education *per se*.

If the influence of official examining bodies and their qualifications is diminished, there is a risk of handing over the selection process to industries or to 'private enterprise' examination bodies, of which there is no dearth in the United States and some of our own management consultancies. In addition to the risk of unofficial dictation of curriculum and school mode by such methods, there are further problems such as ignoring the obsolescence of knowledge, stimulating an artificial demand for continued education in order to get better jobs, and neglecting consideration of the quality of life or the wellbeing of the individual candidate.

Qualities of persistence, creativity, and commitment in students and teachers are underplayed in most patterns of examination already; and the pursuit of diagnostic expertise for what are essentially non-educational purposes has already caused grave concern. Real educational effectiveness is undervalued; not even scholastic 'efficiency' is assured. Systematic studies by OECD in recent years reached the conclusion that no currently available measurements reliably show educational success or long-term effectiveness; (and therefore we lack a measure of schools' most important commitment). New criteria are being earnestly sought.

ARE THERE NEGLECTED CRITERIA FOR EDUCATIONAL EFFECTIVENESS?

Most well-developed countries wish to place increasing emphasis on technologically justifiable preparation, not just in the sense of technical training but including what in the English language are understood as 'professional' attitudes of responsibility, humanity, and social commitment. Few countries have got very far; but among those conspicuously trying are France and Sweden. It has to be admitted that nearly all vocational education is very restricted and restrictive everywhere. No matter what 'general education' it contains, those involved in it very often concentrate on narrow competences. For vocational reasons themselves multiple competences and adaptability are now required – though seldom appreciated by teachers or students in this field. Moreover the 'polytechnical' aspect so assiduously cultivated in the Soviet Union (for example), with every advantage of ministerial manipulation of the schools' life and total control of the mass media of persuasion, has still to contend with bourgeois regard for white collar credentials and life style. It is by such criteria that most learning is appraised, rather than by anything intrinsic or humane.

A long-term objective is to encourage students to look forward to more polyvalent and *personal* skill, and ultimately to much more automation, as the Russians have been doing for more than a decade. A more immediate reaction is to bring technological interests under the same umbrella of school provision and examination formulation as the 'general' parts of the curriculum. That has been done in France with some notable success; but current observation on the ground indicates a deepening and widening cleavage between those newly respectable technological interests and the older, more utilitarian training offered in the *collèges d'enseignement technique* (CET), due for reform after 1975.

The reformative responses just mentioned are nearly all structural or organisational (as the majority of them will continue to be); but important questions remain of widening the conspectus of educational development from within. We must include more awareness of social change, and also break down affective and social barriers between distinguishable types of course, examination, and career. This group of objectives constantly reappears in Swedish approaches to curricular development and the reform of assessment methods. That country's long-term planning even from the industrial side involves reaching out and engaging the workers in school or higher education re-arrangements.

Any such participation of 'outsiders' in the work of education and its appraisal inevitably lowers the 'protection level' for teachers and educational administrators, including those responsible for examinations. The introduction into school objectives and criteria of affective, moral, aesthetic, and social considerations (though they 'humanise' school and also encourage a positive attitude to learning) soon brings confrontation with accepted 'theories of knowledge' and the formalised objectives of curricula and examination systems; yet that move should enlarge the fields of self-expression, self-confidence and resourcefulness in schools and in young adult students themselves.

How such desiderata can be combined with formal systems of examination or other appraisal is a problem unresolved. It is certainly not a problem only for teachers and students, but one requiring national resolution. Nevertheless, it *is* a critical point of decision in which the needs and perceptions of young adults' education *as a whole* are central to successful planning.

3

UPPER-SECONDARY ALTERNATIVES

This chapter will examine a few of the most important alternatives tried out or proposed for upper-secondary education. Our main interest is in the way ahead for post-compulsory education as a whole; but it will be helpful to survey those alternative patterns, or elements within them, which seem most promising for the new relationships required.

With this intent we can look back briefly on the antecedents of present provision for upper-secondary education, because the legacy of past experience and relationships to a great extent influences present attitudes and expectations. After a frank look at what is hidden behind the present we can go on more hopefully to see if there is an effective choice of genuine *alternatives* in the upper-secondary/lower-tertiary range – instead of a hierarchy of first, second, third, and *n*th choices in a descending order of respectability. For only the provision of genuine alternatives enjoying equivalence or 'complementariness' wherever similar attainment levels and learning intensity are achieved will help education systems to satisfy requirements already acknowledged. The very use of the word 'alternative' in this full sense is still unusual.

CAN THERE BE ALTERNATIVES?

Our survey of the present scene has already shown that the search for 'parity of esteem' has usually caused 'modern' courses of study to seek respectability by being admitted within a scheme of examination originally intended for the more traditionally academic kind of institution or course. Either to add substance or simply to lend the trappings of familiar learning, elements like science or modern languages have been added to technical and commercial courses. The process has therefore been one of assimilation or accreditation, rather than of finding real alternatives. Evidence in OECD documents, for example, shows that the characteristically *variant* element in those institutions or courses has often been diminished, since the ultimate intention is the same — namely, to provide admissibility to the *university,* and indeed to the most respectable faculties there.* Therefore, the concealed intention is not educational at all, but occupational and social. The really technical or vocational kind of preparation in such circumstances then has to be sought elsewhere, often in short 'no-nonsense' training courses which in some countries are provided by other Ministries. Obviously they appeal to the poor and educationally underdeveloped; so equivalence of any kind is negated.

The strong association of vocational-technical courses with the 'less able' is an important factor in any discussion today. When under 10% of the over-11s went to any kind of secondary education (as in Britain in 1938), and then only for a short time as a rule, it was understandable that

---

*An excellent survey of the field, and trends until 1970, is presented in A. G. Hearnden, *Paths to University: Preparation, Assessment, Selection* (1973).

vocationally linked courses should seem appropriate to the 'second best' pupils, though by that time several important reports had declared they ought to be equivalent in value for study. Today the successors of those same 'second best' pupils not quite fit for secondary school continue their education and training in the university, if not in postgraduate study, as the simplest comparison of the proportions involved will show. Other countries' experience reinforces the point. So that 'less able' association is spurious. The judgement of 1938 was not educational, but a reflection of the proportions assumed to be necessary for manning the socio-economic structure of those days. Now we need not merely more people better developed, but also better developed in and through those same occupationally oriented courses of study. That is an *educational* observation as well as a statement about manpower.

Another element in the picture should be picked out. Though the present book is concerned with full-time education, it becomes easier to understand problems in the growth of full-time vocationally linked education if we spare a moment for part-time plans. From the end of the first World War many countries (like Britain, France, and Germany) introduced legislation to ensure that those who left full-time schooling before completing the full secondary school period should continue their education and/or training on a part-time basis in publicly provided courses for a few years. Hardly any British local authorities kept this up for long, though the Industrial Training Act of 1964 revived the intention.

In France, however, the provisions of the Loi Astier of 1919 and its special tax support provided a widespread though incomplete system of part-time apprenticeship courses. It later financed some full-time technical supplements to ordinary school provision. Many of these continue in full force; and some of the vocationally linked courses even in *lycées* today draw substantial benefit from the same supply of funds.

In the Federal Republic of Germany, the tradition of the part-time vocational school *(Berufsschule)* with compulsory attendance to the age of 18 for those who have left full-time school has not only continued in full vigour but has given rise also to several types of full-time vocational sequel beyond the age of 16. Among these are the vocational continuation school *(Berufsaufbauschule)* and a wide range of full-time vocational and technical parallels. Some of these are approached from the *Berufsschule;* others usually follow the short-term secondary school *(Realschule* or *Mittelschule)* about the age of 16; and some are beginning to draw students from the academic *Gymnasium* about the same age, though usually the less successful of these.

Within the selective secondary school provision of most continental systems, a great array of 'applied' studies arranged in 'package deal' combinations is usually available for choice from about the age of 14, 15, or 16 according to the country; and some of these are clearly 'commercial', 'technical', or even 'vocational'.* But their names and our own familiar expectations should not deceive us. Two important factors preclude any real equivalence, and remove the possibility of genuinely alternative choices. The first is that these courses, even if within the 'general education' provision of the country, are well understood to be ranged in a descending order of esteem (so much so that teachers will threaten a student with relegation to one further down the list). The second factor is that the institutions or departments

---

*Details of these, in all the countries of the research programme, are given in our earlier book, chapters 5-9.

housing them are officially distinguished in various ways – supervision by different Ministries, 'control' by different examinations, staffing by teachers with poorer qualifications, and usually recruitment of supposedly inferior students. This second factor is aggravated if, as in West Germany, a 'dual system' exists to segregate 'general education' from vocational establishments. It is this parallel and segregated coexistence which has dominated most thinking about the problems of providing possible alternatives in the sense advocated here, especially since the huge expansion of numbers in post-compulsory education has brought so many within sight of higher education and all it may mean professionally.

In countries like those of Western Europe and North America, educational policy has in recent years been motivated by two main concerns: to expand educational and social opportunity by 'democratisation' in various ways; and to improve the manpower potential of those educated in two not always compatible perspectives – those of specific expertise and 'polyvalent' adaptability. 'Polyvalent' adaptability is much the more recently recognised. It is given prominence in this book and its predecessor. Besides, even specific expertise is increasingly seen as provisional both in its own need for further technical development and also in its external need to be 'humanised' by insights from the social field. Both needs affect all career expectations.

PERMANENT OR PERMEABLE STRATIFICATION?

To some extent these requirements are recognised by recent readjustments in universities and some professional education/training schemes, and still more by 'recurrent education' in various forms. But all this is still novel if not suspect in traditional quarters. The demand for specific training, either in some sort of college or school, or within the firm itself, continues to grow. It is not only a question of extending the array of specific skills and specific knowledge, however. Manpower planners see not only perpendicular parallels of specialisation, so to speak; they also see horizontal strata of attainment. French planners, for example, extrapolated from the evidence of the 1960s that skilled personnel would be required for the 1970s on four levels: 10% of the age-group, or 80,000 people, from the *grandes écoles* and universities for the top two levels together; another 10% from people who had two years of education and training beyond the *baccalauréat;* and another 15% from those possessing the *baccalauréat.* (In passing, we note the projection of 35% of the age-group succeeding in the very difficult *baccalauréat*).

In consequence of the expected requirement of a skilled 'intermediate' workforce with two years *beyond* secondary education, the 'university institutes of technology' or IUTs have been developed from 1966 onwards. There had previously been attempts to develop this kind of provision within the universities, but unsuccessfully since the faculties there could not hope to compete with the more prestigious *grandes écoles,* and the faculties' teachers did not want to be bothered with 'lower-level' commitments anyway. At their inception, too, publicity documents made the IUTs seem so accessible to students without their *baccalauréat* that some kind of upper-secondary/lower-tertiary overlap appeared to be envisaged. Similar 'secondary/higher' hybrids have been experimented with elsewhere since the early 1960s, for example in the German Federal Republic and Japan. They are nearly always in the 'higher technician' range, since there is a great shortage of this kind of person. (4 or 5 of them are generally thought to be needed for each 'top technologist'.)

Though these details have intrinsic interest for those concerned with technical and higher education as such, they also demand our attention because they are concrete examples of a much talked of new development – 'short cycle higher education' – in an idiom different from that of the American community college. Not only in the technological and commercial field, but in other applied and general studies of many kinds, there are significant developments in the upper-secondary/lower-tertiary range which not only satisfy some manpower needs immediately but illustrate a more important long-term prospect – that of gradually extending upper-secondary and post-secondary 'applied' studies which are in close touch with the workaday world yet do not cut students off from further chances of self-development, professional or academic. In other words, they imply a promise of much more 'permeability'.

Let us pursue that idea a little further. The English language speaks of 'access' (as though to heaven) and 'acceptability' (as though to the guardian at the gate). 'Permeability' implies openness not only to people with the right credentials or a tolerated second-best but to ideas, interests, and experiences which do not have to be legitimated by some formal authority. Our continental colleagues are very strong on formal credentials and juridical status. (The school-leaving certificate traditionally gives the *right* to enter the university, for example). The formal ticket after the requisite course will open the specified door on the appropriate level, as in the French plan. Such specialisations are mutually exclusive from the point of entry, and are often prevented from being real alternatives because of entry requirements.

'Permeability' implies something much closer to the intentions of this book: the possibility of attaining competence at a particular level required or desired, without too many demands on previous experience (often a matter of accident, or birth), and with no barriers on further progress beyond currently proved ability to profit. It is implied in the establishment of comprehensive schools, in open-access sixth form colleges, and so forth. It is increasingly accommodated even in universities, both at the initial admission stage and in the possibility of transfer between courses or units. In one individual's study programme it is encouraged by the opportunity to include elements from various fields of study, or at different levels. In some of the new experimental 'short cycle institutions' the opportunity to catch up, begin afresh, or transfer in one of these ways is already actualised.

But how can the 'polyvalent' adaptability of persons and institutions so obviously capable of being developed in the way just described be provided at the same time as highly specific technical/vocational training? That is one question which will recur throughout this chapter and later; but one indication can be given immediately. Institutions already exist in Britain and abroad where specialised courses are provided in parallel for different people, who nevertheless do learn many kinds of 'polyvalence' through living and learning together (perhaps even in formal provision of joint courses or activities). Study courses too are now already in being which are 'short-term' in fulfilling particular study or training requirements, yet 'long-term' in allowing later extension or transfer after gaining the short-term diploma or other qualification. Some new 'half-way' credentials of this kind have been designed with 'permeability' in mind. At the same time, an increasing number of short-term diploma schemes (the Dip.H.E. in England and the D.E.U.G. in France, for example) put the accent on broad foundations before professional specialisation.

'PROVISIONAL' DIFFERENTIATION

If, therefore, specialisation in a group of studies or a form of training is required, neither those who receive the instruction nor those who provide it should nowadays suppose that any permanent classification has been made — either vertically between subject interests or horizontally between levels of attainment. As we saw, the expansion of higher education and the still greater elaboration and expansion of the skilled professions have shown how mistaken it was to suppose that some sort of definable limit restricted either the further development of people or their lateral adaptability. If limits exist, they will doubtless be found by the people themselves who attempt to pursue study or by their teachers and professional selectors on the job. Whatever verdict is reached may be valid for one pursuit, or one time, or one temporary level of attainment — perhaps for only one particular mode of learning whatever should be learned.

This *'prima facie'* position is increasingly recommended to educators at all ages and levels. At the immediately post-compulsory level on which the young adult finds himself ready for a fresh start as a new 'volunteer', willingness to accept a provisional candidate for a proposed course of study or training is obviously most important. What has been said in the past few pages therefore carries clear implications for our evaluation of the expedients that have been tried in upper-secondary/lower-tertiary education at this age- and attainment-level. We can therefore continue our consideration of alternatives from the standpoint already reached by up-to-date thinking and experimentation, instead of relying on older criteria for upper-secondary 'alternatives' which never really counted them as genuine alternatives or at best judged them to be only stages on the way to fully alternative futures. While acknowledging the existence of real or supposed differences in attainment (perhaps ability), and the need to provide variously for them, we do not 'box them up' in permanently separated compartments.

NEED ALTERNATIVES (OR NEWCOMERS) BE CULTURALLY INFERIOR?

Since long before the second World War, reformers have tried to incorporate into a 'real secondary education' a genuinely alternative range with more practically oriented instruction, which could be a vehicle for personal development as well. But for whom? Only for the 'poor achievers'? Only for the newcomers from less successful homes and schools? In those days some of the advocacy of genuine alternatives seemed less realistic than now, perhaps, because now we are talking in very different circumstances. We know now that no categories of occupation and/or knowledge are permanently definable. We recognise that no one category or supposed level of expertise can tell the whole tale, or justifiably lay down the law for others. We are, more importantly, dealing with the average learner as well as the carefully groomed specialist — and both at the level of upper-secondary education. Access to full 'humanity' is a birthright.

Therefore the questions we ask are different from those which seemed reasonable two decades ago. Then the provision of 'equal opportunity' for newcomers was sometimes thought of almost like providing emergency seats in the same establishment, with little basic variation of the curriculum and methods used. Traditional students would experience no change. People still wonder if a larger sixth form intake simply means watering down the curriculum for them or making it less demanding by being 'practical' and 'popular'. (The French call this process *vulgarisation*). Should an easier path be provided for the 'non-traditional' student and those thought unlikely to stay long at that level of education (as the Schools Council Working Party on the 16-19 age-group envisaged)?

Despite that Working Party's recognition that there really is a continuum of ability in the 'new sixth', and that the oft-quoted 'traditional — non-traditional' distinction is mythological, nearly all proposed alternatives for the enlarged post-compulsory enrolment seem to classify an increasing proportion as incapable by nature or upbringing of doing what really matters in formal education. Though incapacity may be true (or partly true) in a minority of cases, it is far from proved of the majority.

In any event, such a judgement deflects attention from the essential questions: whether the traditional upper-secondary curriculum and style genuinely cultivate for anyone the fields of learning now required; whether familiar but expanding areas of knowledge might require presentation in novel ways (to include not merely new knowledge but subtler perceptions and new skills); whether some upper-secondary studies might require a different structure or periodicity for practical reasons (e.g. by coming after work-experience or alternating with it, or by being arranged with a 'modular' structure or according to the attainment profile of individual students); whether important but not easily 'teachable' curricular components like morality and aesthetic development and social competence should be re-thought as *experiential* elements to be learned by all students in common; and what might be done about education in 'the humanities', whether old or new, for that majority of the young adult population which so far has had little benefit of formal education.

This kind of conscience-searching, asking common questions across the whole of the after-16 provision, has been developing apace during the past decade or so. It means very much more than attempting to incorporate technical, commercial, or other 'modern' parallels within the classical secondary framework – all with a view to formal equivalence of some sort. The general change of intellectual and social climate had much to do with this questioning; but two clearly scholastic factors were influential. These were: growing comprehensive school provision in the lower-secondary range before the age of 16; and the rapid expansion of learning horizons opened up for an enlarged post-compulsory population by continuous occupational change. New careers and studies attract the able too.

A SHIFT OF OFFICIAL INTEREST IN THE OVER-16s

The investigations of the Comparative Research Unit at King's College from 1970 onwards certainly seemed to its members to break new ground at a number of points. It was very clear from public discussions during the preceding decade that some member countries of the Council of Europe (for example) keenly opposed the blurring of traditional distinctions between 'general' and 'applied' kinds of education at any level – especially beyond compulsory attendance. They were opposed to removing distinctions between the types of examination associated with particular kinds of curriculum or teaching. They could not contemplate the implied merger of teacher types, or consequential changes in higher education. And if Ministries could accept such prospects with equanimity, the institutions and organisations within their countries were often ferociously opposed (as some still are). It was against this background that the research programme began which gave rise to this book and its predecessor. It was necessary, but not easy, to prepare the way carefully. Despite the welcome we received, there was some persistent scepticism.

Yet after 1968 especially the time was ripe for a huge shift of official interest in the over-16s. In 1971 the seventh conference of the European Ministers of Education decided that their next conference two years later should be on the theme of educating the 16-19 age-group. All member countries were invited to provide reports on their existing provision and any concrete changes expected by 1973. For the first time, all types of upper-secondary education were thus included in a single official overview, with no implication that unsullied 'general education' was essentially distinguishable from workaday interests, let alone superior. The conference's brief was novel, too, in including some students over the theoretical age limit but nevertheless undergoing upper-secondary education appropriate to that age-range.

The country reports are included in *The Educational Needs of the 16-19 Age Group* (CME-HF (73) 1). An analytical treatise by Professor Henri Janne and M. l'Inspecteur Général L. Géminard, with the same title (1973), already referred to in this book, presented sociological and pedagogical considerations arising from the country reports. It drew on the conclusions of an earlier symposium on pre-university education (1972), reported in the Council of Europe document CCC/EGT (72) 1. That symposium criticised upper-secondary schools as places generally cut off from life, silent, discriminatory, favouring the 'noble' branches of learning, and marked by passivity, irresponsibility, and repeated failure.

Janne and Géminard accepted that one or more of the

criticisms could be applied to some or nearly all such schools according to the evidence officially provided in the country reports, and from other sources. They recognised that instead of simply accepting the school-certificate-university or school-diploma-job syndrome, educational systems must come to terms with the actuality of new learning conditions, constantly changing social and occupational requirements, and a very different kind of student expectation. They emphasised the need for a comprehensive overview of the *sub-culture in and around the schools.* 'This environment is an "educational" reality, and one of the factors which must be taken into account in any educational and cultural policy.' The authors italicised that passage, and went on to say (again in italics): 'Any reform of the educational system which claimed to be based only on "school" data would be in danger of dealing with the symptoms and not with the aetiology of the disease'.

About the same time (in 1971-1972) G. Vincent, with the help of some of his students, conducted a mainly out-of-school investigation of over 6,000 pupils and students in Paris, which resulted in the publication of *Le Peuple Lycéen* (1973). Great care was taken in that survey to examine the views of students in less privileged institutions and also out of school altogether, as well as of *lycéens* proper. That book commands attention not only for its vivid first-hand information from questionnaires and interviews but also for a remarkable collection of parallel statements from student journals, manifestos, and some public policy papers.

In the great ferment of ideas and debates after 1968, discussion took many unrelated forms. Much student opinion in schools as well as higher education was expressed in directly political terms of confrontation, reciprocated by shock and indignation on the other side. Some official political-administrative disquiet took the form of developing parallel or otherwise reformed structures in school or higher education, both to provide modern alternatives in the study programmes and to give teachers and students more say in the conduct of educational affairs. The 'say' was often political or personal rather than educational, though some excellent ideas were voiced and printed. Philosophical and pedagogical principles were brandished with apostolic zeal across a great divide. A large number of conferences were held, sometimes on parallel themes and disparate levels, often too in idioms which were conceptually foreign to each other. Practically never, however, was post-compulsory education considered in general terms – and almost never with any representation of the 'inside view' before the great *Colloque National* of late 1973.*

We were therefore fortunate in undertaking our main fieldwork at this time (from 1971 onwards) after close discussion with colleagues in the Ministries and research centres concerned. The very readiness to seek alternatives – even on the ground level, and especially in those centres where no consultation of any kind had ever taken place – was favourable to our enquiries. (At least it was favourable when respondents learned that we did not represent the Ministry.) Yet in these circumstances the question of alternatives (even within their own establishment or elsewhere in their national system) was for many respondents like consideration of foreign territories and life-styles – not really about reform through a *system* of complementary alternatives for the future in a generically new style of upper-secondary education.

---

*Recorded in 2 volumes of the *Actes du Colloque National sur l'Education, November 21-23, 1973* (Paris, 1974).

NEW IDEAS? NEW STRUCTURES? OR BOTH?

Evidently the shift of official interest in the over-16s as a whole, and the increasing amount of documentation from every source after 1968, have so far failed to pervade general consciousness in the schools and colleges. It was astonishing to find that on the one hand a few pioneering thinkers in Ministries and research centres had a broad understanding of the developing educational future which was shared not only by scholars outside 'Education' but by some student leaders (as their documents show), while on the other hand most formally professional educators so often restricted their gaze to structural reorganisation or curricular plumbing. That is, if they were willing to consider change at all. Reluctance to change was not always ascribable to lack of sensitivity. More often, perhaps, it reflected undue concern for customs of pedagogy which were believed to represent 'values' of some sort, like the minute study of texts and theories — but with little reference to alternative values accorded priority in a different educational world.

Nevertheless, structural changes in school and college systems and reorganisation of the curriculum and examinations connected with them did represent one possible means of reconciling new needs with familiar establishments. By 'establishments' in this context we mean not only schools and colleges, or the well ordered structure of the teaching profession in most countries, but the evaluation and job-accreditation systems inseparable from them. It is bound to take years before A-Levels in Britain and their counterparts abroad lose popular prestige or job-winning usefulness, no matter what educational pundits may say about the desirability *and utility* of 'participant' learning and generic educational newness. All the same, these things can be developed (and slowly are being developed) within the structural framework of new institutional and curricular alternatives (perhaps the best practical move), without loss of favourite credentials and preoccupations for the time being. The ideological shift of interest we speak of is still so very new that acceptance may be slow.

Of course, many of the ideas discussed in these pages were already 'in the air', especially from the mid-1960s onwards (i.e., before 1968); but it is only very recently indeed that they have been pulled together. We are proud to have shared in that process with perceptive and sometimes illustrious colleagues whose contributions we are glad to quote, as well as with our generous respondents. Yet satisfaction that the ferment of discussion continues should not obscure the recency of that discussion, and the corresponding uncertainty that surrounds its practical outcome. The discussion needs to be taken much further, of course; and the evidence must still be sought and gathered all around. The real examination of post-compulsory education as a whole is still at a very early stage.

The practical outcome just referred to includes much more than ideal programming. The pressure mounts to find places for students immediately. The need to improvise as well as plan ahead in curriculum development and deployment of resources focuses the attention of teachers and administrators very narrowly. No matter what the external wisdom and support, adaptation is often hasty and *ad hoc.* Not all re-thinking therefore is of the abstract kind, but expressed in very corporate form. At least the British scene provides many sound examples of empirical imagination, with reorganisation of structure and course-work not only to respond to some novel idea but to provide a matrix in which new ideas may be generated.

In the light of today's new educational commitments it would be wrong to look only or mainly to structural modification, or to be content with the classifications, hierarchies, and allocations which any head of institution might devise – no matter how well alerted. Inevitably, structures and their relationships are only 'interim statements' in concrete form of someone's vision of the whole, and its functional interactions. For the future, all of that must be provisional. The most interesting point about British arrangements is that experimentation in that new perspective is so easy.

OPPORTUNITIES FOR VARIETY IN BRITISH POST-COMPULSORY EDUCATION

To understand the picture fully it should be made clear that the selective grammar schools in England and Wales have never been uniformly selective. The percentage of 11-year-olds accepted by the schools has varied from about 12½% to over 40% according to time and location. For that reason and others, the range of subjects studied has varied from a restricted group to a wide range of interests. As already noticed, the development of combined schools (e.g. bilateral and comprehensive) has meant internal changes of character. Yet it has usually been supposed that the 'sixth form' (the last 2 or 3 years) would maintain high academic standards with a very strong university expectation.

However, Mr. A. D. C. Peterson in *The Future of the Sixth Form* (1973) showed that less than one-third of even 'traditional' sixth-formers go to university; almost a quarter go straight into employment; nearly one-third of the traditional sixth-formers get only one A-Level or none; and an increasing proportion of the 'non-traditional' students do not take the examination at all. So it cannot be imagined that the sixth form even in favoured selective schools should be judged for formal efficiency by the criterion of A-Level performance.

When we also take account of a few figures from the Schools Council Working Paper No. 45 of 1972 (Table 16) we face a real challenge. Starting with an actual figure of about 312,700 sixth-formers in school in 1970 ('traditional' students and otherwise), the Working Party predicted a possible 525,000 'traditional' sixth-formers by 1981, while the figure for 'non-traditional' enrolments was 'not available'. Despite a recent lowering of estimates, reliable evidence suggests that upper-secondary enrolment figures might be very large indeed. That consideration alone, as well as educational re-thinking, has already made many local education authorities arrange alternative accommodation in special sixth-form units, 'sixth-form secondary colleges', and several kinds of hybrid or new institutions, sometimes under 'further education' auspices.

Accommodating large numbers in school systems intended for a much smaller enrolment obviously causes problems of teacher supply and course provision. Any decision to hive off some or all of the over-16s gives an opportunity to re-think in other ways. One apparently trivial change of terminology may be significant. Statistics from the Department of Education and Science divide the school population into 'boys' and 'girls'; yet those in further education *of the same age* are classified as 'men' and 'women' if they are over 15.

Between 1966 and 1970 the percentage of students obtaining their A-Level *in further education colleges* doubled — as a proportion *of a greatly increased A-Level total,* as we saw above. Further education colleges now provide a rapidly increasing proportion of all university entrants. It is clear therefore that the junior part of many further education colleges (which they now usually call their 'tertiary' level to distinguish it from 'higher' courses) has become an obvious alternative to traditional sixth forms even where the latter continue to exist. There is a growing migration from the secondary schools of every type to the further education colleges for a variety of reasons: because of a more mature atmosphere; because of specialised teaching and facilities in many cases; because of tedium with school; because of the need for a fresh start; to gain the opportunity of new combinations of subject and other interests; to meet the other sex under more normal conditions (many English secondary schools are still single-sex institutions); and to meet people from different walks of life, including some who are mature and have had experience of paid employment or perhaps raising a family.

Four sixth-form 'secondary' colleges of the separated type were included in the English part of the research survey. In one of the towns visited, the sixth form college has since been combined with part of the 'further education' provision to form a new establishment. Some towns have distinct types in co-existence; others have abolished sixth forms altogether and concentrated post-compulsory work in further education colleges. Other local authorities display a wide range of 'consortia' with sharing of facilities, sharing of schools (especially boys' with girls' schools), and linked-course schemes whereby students are enrolled and find a home on one school or college base but take part of their work at another. Every scheme has its champions and critics, thus providing an extremely active workshop-cum-forum for this age-range in British education.

Some sixth-form colleges are selective in the sense that they require those admitted to have obtained four subject-certificates in the General Certificate of Education (Ordinary Level) at about the age of 16 before they come. Others are completely open in the matter of entry qualifications. Both open and selective systems generally offer a wide range of curricular choices, though the non-selective institutions range more widely. An advantage of re-organisation after 16 is to be found in this wide choice of options. Success is very often achieved by students whose admission attainment did not seem promising. In 1973 only 23 separate sixth-form colleges or junior colleges existed; 60 were established by the end of 1974, and more were planned for opening soon. In addition, 5 local education authorities had concentrated their 'sixth-form' provision in a total of 9 colleges of further education. If hybrids and combined arrangements are taken into account the number is much greater. Of 132 LEAs which had their reorganisation plans approved by the Department of Education and Science in a 1972 survey, 51 authorities had even then introduced or proposed some kind of concentrated sixth-form provision. Of course, such figures fail to indicate the increasing voluntary migration of young adults to the further education colleges available in their vicinity.

These changes, bringing more local comprehensiveness into the over-16 level, introduce a fresh advantage which may not be suspected, namely that of community attachment. By the nature of the selective process, an academic secondary school draws its pupils from an ever-expanding geographical district in proportion as selection becomes more intense. One such school in our survey, for example, then received half its intake from outside the rather large town in which it is situated. (That policy has now been altered.) Nearly all those initially enrolled at the age of 11 went on into the sixth form. There they were joined by about an equal number of newcomers satisfying the entry requirements, of whom less than half came from the same town. A notable proportion of the new recruits had previously attended independent, rather than maintained, schools. So the local education authority had been maintaining a very good school and excellent

facilities to serve not only a wide geographical area but a
body of students by no means representing growth in local
maintained schools. The educational loss to the local
community and the community loss to the students
themselves are clearly obvious.

Some of the pitfalls inherent in developing a selective but
'mushroom' sixth form are well revealed by the illustration
just given. It is by no means uncommon for a single enlarged
sixth form (as part of an existing school) to recruit a few
newcomers from a number of feeder schools around. That
system seems economical, perhaps, until large numbers begin
to stay on beyond 16. Then questions arise about
accommodating the steady onward flow of students in the
post-compulsory phase. Separate *ad hoc* provision then looks
administratively attractive. The argument against detaching
the post-16 phase on the ground that it marks a break in the
continuity of school life (which for many may be a distinct
advantage) looks even less convincing when we recognise that
any sixth form receiving a large inflow from other
establishments is already a very much altered environment
for those who stay on from the same school. In addition, it is
a new and separate place for all the newcomers.

In any case, as already shown, no 'traditional' sixth form
can claim to be unaltered in our time. The very enlargement
of a sixth form's numbers even from its own lower school,
together with a widening range of career interests, personal
expectations, and outside contacts, necessarily transforms the
sixth form's character in ways for which the existing school
and staff are seldom prepared.

Consequently several reasons justify the provision of a
really 'young adult' fresh start in different circumstances in a
special place, notably for some students or in particular local
circumstances. Questions of accommodation and economical
use of facilities may thereby be resolved. The wish for a move

revealed in young adults' spontaneous migration to further education establishments is met. More than scholastic opportunities are enhanced, since social and humane benefits are sometimes obvious. Yet it is surprising how tenaciously some British local education authorities persist in regarding schools as quite separate from further education, and indeed segregating school from school (especially boys from girls) when the students' own out-of-school contacts are more realistic.

Nearly all headmasters and headmistresses of secondary schools campaign rather fiercely against any 'lopping' of their sixth forms, frequently with the absolute sincerity of educational conviction. However, those who have experienced such a change almost always express full satisfaction with the separate sixth form or sixth form college development. Former problems of discipline, motivation, and human relationships are said to have disappeared. With so much experimentation going on it would be premature to draw definitive conclusions; but the pointers are significant. Let us attempt a perspective of relevant developments.

THE ENGLISH SIXTH FORM COLLEGE

When R. Wearing King published his book of that title (Pergamon, 1968), he subtitled it 'An educational concept'. It was he who, as Chief Education Officer of Croydon in 1954, first really argued the case for a college to supersede the existing boys' and girls' grammar school sixth forms in the town (five in number, not counting independent schools), and to bring them together in a properly staffed and equipped establishment. Problems of staffing the existing sixth forms adequately, and avoiding waste of scarce resources, were seen by some as the real reason behind the move; but no one who saw these proposals from the beginning or who has read the retrospective book reviewing all the issues and experiments to which 'The Croydon Plan' gave rise can doubt its innovative force.

However, that plan was rejected on what now looks like very bad expert advice. Lord Crowther, formerly Chairman of the Central Advisory Council for Education which produced the 1959 Report on *15 to 18,* wrote in a preface to Wearing King's book that 'The teaching profession, for reasons which I fear reflect no credit on it, has succeeded in putting a virtually complete ban on the whole idea'. At the time the book was published (1968) there were only two publicly financed sixth form colleges; and of these only Mexborough had been deliberately planned as such. What Lord Crowther called 'this shameful prejudice' against the sixth form college has by no means broken down; but it has given place to fear (on the part of secondary teachers, mainly) of the scholastic and professional consequences of substituting a college structure for a school sixth form. There is also prejudice on the part of some school governors and individual members of local education authorities. A few of these protesters have seriously read round the issue and learned the necessary facts; but only a minority of those resisting the change show evidence of understanding the *educational* nature of the change proposed or recognising the constructive trend of which it forms part. Widespread discussions have reinforced this book's authors in that verdict, which is corroborated by English evidence in the OECD *Case Studies of Educational Innovation: At the Regional Level* and *At the School Level* (1974). Fortunately, opposition is diminishing, as the growing number of colleges shows.

The first sixth form college was opened in 1966. The first 'tertiary' college for the over-16s based upon a college of further education was inaugurated at Exeter in 1970. As shown earlier, there were 60 of the first type and 9 of the second type in operation at the time of writing, with very many more in the pipeline. In addition, 'sixth form units' enjoying a distinctively more adult style have been developed as integral parts of several secondary schools; and the proportion of those voluntarily transferring to colleges of further education grows steadily. In short, administrators are by-passing theoretical arguments against change, while the young adults themselves increasingly 'vote with their feet' for studies and relationships of college type.

Though many local authorities decided in principle for colleges, ministerial procrastination before 1973 held up the actual establishment of several and restricted the logical thinking-through of what was entailed locally. Larger-scale consideration of the college system's achievements and potential has been slow until recently. Meanwhile, the usual cry of 'wait and see' is already 20 years old in England; our native evidence is mounting in all kinds of colleges and hybrid school-colleges; student preference is cumulatively clear; and the parallel deliberations and investigations of ministries and research centres abroad tell an unmistakable tale. So do OECD and the Council of Europe's expert committees and conferences.

Besides, firm evidence is now to hand. *Post-Compulsory Education I: A New Analysis in Western Europe* gives over 100 tables illustrating English students' learning experience and aspirations, or their teachers' perception of the same, together with tabulation of curricular provision in various types of English secondary schools or colleges at this age-range, as well as verbal analyses of mainly English evidence in a majority of the chapters. This evidence is strongly reinforced by other Western European findings reported elsewhere. Surveys by the National Foundation for

Educational Research, and collateral reports from university research centres or individual school or college projects, leave no doubt of *young adult students'* substantially different place in today's educational thinking. Their insights as well as expectations have won welcome and recognition far beyond the schools.

To take but one example: the Associated Examining Board (concerned here with *Ordinary*-Level General Certificates of Education) reported in 1974 that its 'alternative scheme' of special investigations undertaken by students in sixth forms and equivalent levels of technical colleges had produced original work of surprisingly high quality outside the candidates' normal studies, winning the acclaim of experts in some cases. Consequently, the scheme was extended to some 2,000 students. We cannot be surprised at this intellectual maturity when we reflect once more that at 18 students can vote, marry without parental consent, own property and (in some countries) be conscripted. At the age of 16 they can help to elect works councils and boards of management. When they are 18 they can serve on boards of governors for schools and technical colleges, and when scarcely older they can sit on university senates or committees. Yet in many schools (including some in our survey) teachers still refer to their over-16s as 'children'. Can we wonder that so many opt for an over-16 college?

English sixth form colleges generally enrol between about 300 and 800 students. Those with selective entry (4 O-Levels as a rule) mainly retain the examination objectives characteristic of similar sixth forms, though often in a much wider range of subjects at A-Level. Experience shows that development after 16 can be very rapid, so that many colleges start some A-Level courses from scratch for beginners. A much more common feature is to allow students to expand their range by adding new O-Level interests.

Colleges with 'open admission' often do all these things too — with notable success; and they generally provide a large range of opportunities to begin, continue, or repeat studies to O-Level for those who have not succeeded so far. So do colleges of further education. An important background factor is that 'feeder' schools may not be well staffed, may not have offered the subject now sought, may have 'timetabled' it out of the student's reach, or may have failed to arouse interest.

A strong effort is usually made to provide each student with a study-plan tailored to his needs and attainments — an individual plan, if possible. Emphasis is generally placed on 'minority' studies outside a chosen specialised range; and common studies in as many 'humanity' interests as possible are encouraged. Private study and community activities feature strongly. Student-managed coffee bars and clubs are frequently found. Student representatives on a college council exercise varying amounts of influence on college life. Tutorial groups and personal tutor systems are usual. Counselling provision varies; its special difficulties and its needs for the future are discussed at the end of this chapter.

No hard-and-fast description could be given, for two main reasons: there is so much local variation, accentuated by the carry-over of the head's autonomy from the English secondary school tradition; and that variation is increased still further by the differences in experience provided by the 'feeder' schools. Individuality in the new colleges is marked, too, by the fact that a few are still single-sex establishments while others are mixed; some have fairly close ties (e.g., through a students' union) with local colleges of further education; and others are associated in one of the 'consortia' increasingly developed to pool resources and/or social advantages. Yet these detailed differences matter far less than the common recognition of a new *genre* of education with a sense of fresh purpose. When we reflect that most college principals and teachers previously served in selective secondary schools – and that many of them too were apprehensive when the change-over began – the extent and intensity of the conversion already achieved is remarkable.

One point of some consequence for Britain must be repeated here. Most sixth form colleges or junior colleges so far developed in England receive nearly all their intake straight from schools. It can be doubted whether that will be true in a few years' time. Doubtless, more students will have had working experience, and more will be 'catching up' – perhaps after family life, perhaps after a change of study choice – but still at about the same attainment level. Special staff preparation, in-service development, and different facilities may be called for.

At this point there is no profit in giving details of curricular provision, to which a whole section of our previous book is devoted, and on which summary recommendations are made in the final chapter of the present book. The essentials have already been made clear. No matter what curriculum is apparently provided, young adults will derive different curricular experience from it. Ideally, that personal profile should suit them, spark or sustain interest, and put them in contact with other people and further studies. Each study programme should be personalised for the individual, yet broadly-based and 'socialised' enough to promote a community of discourse.

The authors accept the general desirability of many others' recommendations: in particular, for a general minimum range of about 5 subjects or fields of interest (with benefit of counselling), to include communication skills and cultivate the affective, moral, and aesthetic aspects of humanity. Decision-sharing and interdependence need to match a growing sense of discovery and autonomy. These desiderata have been in part translated into subject categories by others (e.g., in the Schools Council Working Party Paper No. 45, pages 58 and 60) and into other curricular components by ourselves (as in the final chapter). Yet these tactical dispositions merely serve the new strategy for post-compulsory education. In their turn they depend for effectiveness on continuing feedback from the students and the teachers who learn and re-learn with them.

NEW ALTERNATIVES AND EXPERIMENTS OVERSEAS

The community colleges of the United States have already been mentioned. They provide first steps in post-secondary education (US 'higher education') locally, in a wide range of interests, and serve many age- and attainment-levels. Mainly, they retain their original purpose of providing for those just over 18; but it seems fair to note the possible utility of their example for British over-16s because in many states they follow immediately after compulsory school attendance, and make provision for 'returners' too. Community or junior colleges in typical American circumstances combine secondary-school completion with vocational training, 'short-cycle higher education', adult education, and community facilities for recreation and the arts. This catalogue does not necessarily suggest a similar role for the sixth form college or junior college in Britain; but it does not rule it out either, especially as expert policy documents and recommendations from the Labour and Liberal parties during 1973 look in a similar direction. Multi-purpose provision and multi-media supplementation are likely to feature strongly during the next few decades' expected development of post-compulsory education.

More obviously akin to some British thinking about the over-16s are suggestions from the German Federal Republic and from Scandinavia. Since the end of World War II the Education Ministers of the 11 autonomous *Länder* have slowly agreed on the desirability of establishing some combined arrangement for schools and vocational training institutions (comprehensive 'under one roof', multilateral as a group of units, or co-ordinated in some other way). The Standing Conference of Ministers and the (federal) German Education Council have gradually pressed forward the idea of a combined upper-secondary *system* beyond the age of 16, to efface outmoded distinctions and upgrade vocational preparation. Along these lines the overall education plan *(Bildungsgesamtplan)* passed at the end of 1973 seemed confidently 'comprehensive' in the scholastic sense. Indeed, some of the *Länder* had already established the comprehensive *Kolleg* experimentally or as the keystone of their future. Allowing for differences of idiom and history, this may be roughly compared to a British sixth form college or its further education counterpart.

It is not suggested, of course, that overseas examples of any kind should be *copied*. Their chief value is to present a possible perspective or a fresh framework of analysis which can be helpful if sustained by really reliable evidence. Yet we should know that in several of our neighbour countries very similar problems to our own are being examined and coped with — sometimes in similar ways and sometimes very differently. It is helpful, too, to recognise how frequently forward thinking blurs old distinctions not merely between the contemporary compartments of upper-secondary schools and training courses but between those and 'further' or 'higher' courses where that is appropriate. At least, facilities are provided or proposed so as to allow that to happen.

Following our White Paper of 1972 *(Education: A Framework for Expansion)* and the Circular 7/73 which discussed new roles for colleges of education, the new Diploma in Higher Education seems to have opened up possibilities of much wider extension of 'half-way' provision in institutions of higher education generally. At any rate, the matter has been freely discussed. Precursors of this idea were already to be found in the general introductory courses of some universities, and in the university diplomas established in France since 1966 – also after a two-year course. In this connection, therefore, the *Oberstufenkolleg* at Bielefeld in the German Federal Republic should be mentioned. Despite some furious university opposition this project, experimented with since 1970, combines the last 3 years of school and the university's foundation course, and leads to an intermediate qualification. Its only prerequisites are completion of 10 years' schooling and an age lower than 26.

A long time ago it became possible in Canada to take the first year of university work in school, for 'senior matriculation'. The 1973 Carnegie Report on American higher education made a similar recommendation. The French and the Japanese in different ways have experimented with the same idea, which (in effect) is already put into practice without much publicity in British colleges of further education, where the whole gamut of upper-secondary and undergraduate courses is spanned. There is a range of diplomas whose status is so far indeterminate (i.e., it is not certain whether they have graduate equivalence or not, and for what purposes), and which are doubtless due for rationalisation in a short time. While that is going on, the broader question of providing structurally for new-style upper-secondary/lower-tertiary alternatives should be combined with enquiries about the transition-stages and credentials for further study. In this respect, British example may be very helpful to systems overseas.

Let us pass on to another aspect of providing really effective upper-secondary education – the question of whether it works well and is in tune with the community's expectations generally. Dissatisfaction can take two obvious forms. Most comprehensive school systems have not yet solved problems of inequality of opportunity. Often they attain impressive standards of examination success; yet unrest, absenteeism and destructiveness attract increasing criticism. (That is not, however, confined to non-selective schools.) Something seems to be conceptually wrong with the mixture, which might be cured by ensuring more links in spirit and action with the adult and post-secondary world. School or junior college systems which welcome adults as students, and which are centres for community activities, are already on the way to curing the problem. The post-compulsory phase is then seen to be obviously (as it is educationally) part of a continuum with adult education and the surrounding world. In Britain this sort of move is slowly becoming acceptable, but is still novel. A recent Swedish recommendation, based upon far more extensive experience of such problems (with over 80% 'of the age-group' in schools to the age of about 19), may therefore be of interest.

In Sweden a climax of reorganisation of the upper-secondary phase seemed to have been reached in 1971 with the nation-wide establishment of the comprehensive *gymnasialskole* embracing previously separated 'general' and vocational provision, especially when that was followed by a sweeping overview of traditional and vocationally-linked higher education in the U68 Report of 1973. But an apparently satisfactory structural reorganisation was not enough. Lack of interest among students, truancy, and dropping out have caused many problems. (Among older age-groups *average* absenteeism in the Stockholm district reached 114 periods in an academic year). The proposed devolution of the centralised administrative system has not yet been effective; and the traditional isolation of specialist teachers from general teachers (and from each other) did not help co-ordination. Parental absence from home at the end of school day, single-parent families, and familiar urban disintegration contributed to malaise.

Therefore the Swedish School Structure Commission (SIA) in 1974 proposed to tackle problems lower down the school as well as at the post-compulsory level so as to make school 'a community-oriented open institution . . . a living educational and social centre', involving parents, teachers, and students more closely not only in activities but in management. Teacher-teams, individual and group study programmes, work-links, and much closer utilisation of extra-scholastic persons and resources had already been tried out successfully in 25 experimental centres before the announcement was made; but general implementation, if agreed, would take 10 to 15 years.

However, widening the range of alternatives, keeping the options open, and opening school or college opportunities to 'returners' and to the community at large — all these desirable things increase the area of uncertainty for the young adults on the threshold. That uncertainty inevitably penetrates the compulsory period of schooling too, especially in Britain where custom makes early specialisation the rule.

A decade has already elapsed since the assembled European Ministers of Education resolved to adopt a system of guidance and counselling as a full or partial replacement for examinations proved to be unreliable and educationally unhelpful. That worthy purpose now looks rather limited — because we have greatly expanded awareness of what educational alternatives really mean at this level, and also because we have far more insights into the possibilities of counselling and guidance. Some governments have taken firm steps. In 1970 the French established a National Office for Information on Education and Careers (ONISEP according to its French initials). This is felt by many students, teachers, and parents to be more concerned with straight employment prospects than with orientation and guidance of other kinds; but that is the starting point for many more 'human' innovations. In the United States the principle of guidance and counselling is now universally accepted. In Britain too a beginning has been made; but our students' replies showed that amid present uncertainties many 'crises' remained without adequate help of this kind. Without effective counselling and guidance the whole prospect of real alternatives in post-compulsory education is at worst a delusion, at best hazy.

COUNSELLING AND GUIDANCE: HOW THE CHALLENGE IS BEING MET IN BRITAIN

We have already pointed to some risks in semi-automatic staying on in full-time upper-secondary/lower-tertiary education, especially if no due regard is paid to aptitude or the appropriateness of the subjects studied for personal development and job prospects. Often alternatives are not merely ignored but unknown, and information is not always easy to get. Moreover, in Britain there has been a widespread feeling that counselling and guidance are somehow 'remedial' or for possible misfits. The positive good that these services can do to *average* (or better) students and their teachers was not fully appreciated until the huge expansion of sixth form provision and its multiplicity of alternatives brought all students so many occasions of uncertainty. Fortunately awareness of the importance of counselling and guidance is growing. Accurate, up-to-date, wide-ranging information and advice are recognised to be not only desirable but absolutely vital to successful post-compulsory education, if not earlier.

What steps have been taken so far to meet this need? Let us first look at the way in which ideas about the nature and practice of counselling and guidance have evolved over the last few years. The terms 'counselling' and 'guidance' are so frequently used to describe very different practices and areas of concern that it is worthwhile clarifying what we mean before going any further.

'Counselling' in Britain generally refers to personal counselling, and tends to be problem-oriented. That is to say, a counsellor's services are usually directed towards clarifying, alleviating and if possible solving an individual's difficulties. These may relate to family life, friendships, sexual relationships, school or college work, or future hopes and plans concerning a job or course of study. The situations with which counsellors are most often faced tend to involve family or other personal relationships. Obviously these may (and frequently do) have repercussions on a student's school or college work and future plans. So one could say that distinctions of this sort are invalid and illogical, since a counsellor dealing with one aspect of an individual's life is inevitably involved in other aspects of it too. To some extent this is true; but because counsellors themselves frequently *do* make this distinction and *do not* profess to handle all the inter-related parts of a person's problem themselves, we shall use the distinction in this discussion of counselling and guidance services.

In Britain there is still little general agreement on the principles or theories of counselling. In the United States, for example, this is not the case, as the Schools Council has pointed out.* There, the following principles apply:

a. *Continuity:* The individual should be able to contact the same counsellor over a long period of time so that a real relationship can develop.
b. *Overall concern:* The pupil or student should be considered as a whole. According to this view, counselling is personal *and* educational *and* vocational at the same time.
c. *Active participation:* The individual should be encouraged to make choices and take decisions, and not rely on the counsellor to do so for him.
d. *Combination of teacher and counsellor roles:* In the United States, these are *not* combined, because it is thought to be too difficult to have relationships with a student in both a pedagogic (even authoritarian) and a non-directive sense. However, opinion in Britain tends to favour a combination of roles, as we shall see shortly.
e. *Preventive, not remedial, counselling:* No 'crisis counselling', if possible. Again there is a contrast with the often problem-oriented work of counsellors in Britain.
f. *Co-ordination:* i.e., the counsellor should be in a position to call on the various other resources and services available inside and outside the school or college.

A COMBINATION OF TEACHING AND COUNSELLING ROLES?

We have noted that in England, unlike the United States,

---

*Schools Council Working Paper 15, *Counselling in Schools* (HMSO, 1967).

opinion tends to favour the combination of teaching and counselling roles. Why is this so? Reasons put forward include the following:

a. *Only teachers are in a position to understand a school or college's atmosphere and values.*
   Yet, as the Schools Council points out, op. cit., this argument is not used in relation to the Department of Education and Science's Inspectorate or that of local education authorities.

b. *Non-teaching counsellors may not be readily accepted by the teaching staff or by students and their parents.*
   Obviously, a counsellor needs to be accepted and recognised as part of the school or college; *but* the fact that he or she has clear links with the outside world can be a decided advantage. Why? Because as a result of his or her outside contacts, the counsellor is in a better position to call on external agencies as and when these are required. Also, because these links with the outside world can be just what a student needs if he feels unwilling or unable to reveal his difficulties to someone whom he associates very closely with the world of school or college.

c. *Teaching is the best way to get to know students.*
   But specialist teaching can restrict the number of students one comes across, and also limit the nature of the teaching/learning relationship. That is why teacher/counsellors are sometimes allocated to 'general' or 'social' studies.

d. *Staff shortages.*
   In a situation where teaching resources are scarce, it is often felt that every member of staff should have some teaching duties. This *is* a strong argument; but at the same time there is a very grave shortage of trained counsellors. As the Schools Council again points out:

... if counsellors have first to be teachers, recruitment from any other profession is in effect barred, and every new counsellor will be a part-time teacher lost, not gained.

e. *Teaching and counselling activities do not inevitably clash.* That is of course true, but the fact remains that counselling work does require *time*. So a counsellor's job (already criticised by some as being too ambitious) will be made even harder if he has to subtract some time for teaching.

f. *High cost of providing counsellors.* This cannot be denied, when one considers the outgoings (training, salary, clerical assistance and accommodation). Yet, even so, can we afford *not* to have trained counsellors in our upper-secondary schools and colleges?

COUNSELLING IN ENGLAND: PRACTICES AND PROBLEMS

Our own research in English schools and colleges found that in most cases a 'personal tutor' system operated whereby full-time teaching staff combined counselling with their teaching duties. Generally, students were divided up into groups of between fifteen and twenty, and then assigned to a personal tutor. Sometimes allocation was deliberately arbitrary; sometimes attempts were made to ensure that a student's tutor or counsellor also taught him or her.

Schools and colleges varied considerably in their views on this matter. Even so, the overall impression was that the staff concerned believed strongly that it was an advantage for a tutor/counsellor to be a teacher at the same time. They felt the advantages in knowing a student personally far outweighed the problems that might arise. Yet the combination of teaching and counselling was not without its problems. Chief among these were: Time; Accommodation; Liaison; and Training.

Time

Staff frequently complained that their teaching duties left them insufficient time for their counselling or tutorial work. Consequently the latter often had to be fitted into coffee- and lunch-breaks, and after school or college hours. Some schools and colleges made timetable provision for counselling activities, but this was often less than one hour per week — far too little time to see students individually. To overcome this problem, some tutor-counsellors made a practice of seeing students in the evening or at weekends, and often invited students to their home. Most felt, though, that their task would be even harder if they did not have a chance to get to know students through teaching them. Staff in sixth form colleges sometimes found their task of building up a relationship with students formidable, given the short period of time available. Yet they felt it was essential if they were to be effective counsellors.

Accommodation

This was seen as another major problem. Staff felt that not only was their work being handicapped by a shortage of time, but also by a lack of suitable accommodation. Often there was nowhere for a tutor and student to meet for a private and confidential discussion — a corridor or classroom is hardly a conducive atmosphere. So tutors were almost unanimous in asking for a room specifically for their counselling work. They felt that this was not only desirable but absolutely essential.

Liaison

Many tutors' comments revealed an underlying anxiety and uncertainty about the boundaries of their responsibilities — the point at which they should hand over to external specialists, and the way in which this should be done. They were anxious not to interfere in the activities of external welfare services, and were only too aware of the need for *co-operation* rather than competition; yet they also felt that there was a need for more co-operation within school or college, so that all those concerned with the welfare of an individual student were fully in the picture.

One tutor put it like this:

> More liaison between those involved in the overall education of the young person, inside/outside the school situation, to establish patterns of working, limits, etc.; dangers of working in one's own boxes; need to recognise confidentiality but to share information so as to prevent too many people becoming involved in the same person's problem.

Training

Even though staff generally believed that their teaching role helped them in their counselling work, many conceded that their lack of training was a very real problem. Often they felt completely out of their depth when faced with students' serious personal and family difficulties. As one tutor remarked:

I think it is imperative that every school counsellor is fully trained and qualified. It seems that many people dabble in this work and merely deal with the tip of the iceberg, unaware that the great bulk of it is submerged and is the real cause of the trouble.

Yet trained counsellors remain a rare breed in English schools and colleges. We found one in only two of the institutions in which we worked. Counselling in Britain is still mainly a part-time and amateur activity. This factual statement is not intended solely as a criticism. Sympathetic, perceptive and sensitive teachers who know their students and who are given the necessary time and facilities can do valuable counselling work. Our own research revealed that a friendly ear was often all that was needed by students, who wished to talk through their problems and anxieties.

Certainly the question of *approachability* is relevant here. Obviously students with serious personal difficulties may wish to remain anonymous and will be more inclined to approach an official counsellor with whom they have had no previous contact, and who appears to be one step removed from the world of school or college. Students might be totally unwilling or unable to discuss their problems with a teacher they know. Yet striking a balance can be difficult. If counsellors remain *too* remote from the day-to-day world of school or college students, they run the risk of appearing to be unapproachable. Certainly our research in Sweden found that trained, non-teaching, counsellors sometimes remained in none-too-splendid isolation; there was little evidence of students' beating a path to their door.

We still have a long way to go in the provision of counselling services. But the first — and arguably most important — step has already been taken. Awareness of the need to provide these services has grown enormously in recent years, and so has the effort to meet this need. It still seems unlikely that the provision of full-time, trained counsellors will become widespread in the near future, and indeed one could argue against the need for this in any case.

Our own research looked in some detail at the part-time, amateur type of counselling service described so far. Our findings suggested that these teacher-counsellors were faced mainly with personal and family problems. Sometimes worried by the risk of becoming too 'involved' and anxious about their competence, they nevertheless provided students with a great deal of friendly advice and support. If and when the problem became too big for them to deal with, they could hand over to external specialists. Often all that was needed was a sympathetic ear and sound common-sense. On this level, one could argue that they achieve a higher degree of success than their trained official counterparts, although on the level of serious personal problems there is a very strong case in favour of the latter.

PROVIDING EDUCATIONAL GUIDANCE AND CAREERS GUIDANCE

Let us now turn to *guidance* services: i.e., the provision of information and advice on educational and employment matters which might affect career prospects and the choice of courses of study. We acknowledge that there is an argument against considering personal counselling separately from guidance in this sense, on the grounds that personal, educational and employment aspects are linked and cannot logically be separated. But because *in practice* the responsibilities for personal counselling *are* often separated from those of careers and educational guidance, we feel justified in maintaining the distinction.

We have already suggested that at a certain level, effective personal counselling can be provided by staff with little or no training. But this is *not* so in the case of careers and educational guidance. Why? Because of the quite different nature of the information and advice involved.

What of the factual background? We have already looked at some of the ways in which educational and job opportunities for young people have changed in recent years. Whole new areas of opportunity have emerged, while others have declined; and there are frequent fluctuations both in the demand for particular skills and in prospects for those with various types and levels of qualifications. At this point it is again worth emphasising the interrelationship between educational guidance and careers guidance. The one cannot be considered in isolation from the other, because educational choices have occupational implications, and vice versa. Indeed, problems often stem from the fact that this relationship has been overlooked.

Within the field of guidance proper, several developments in recent years are of particular significance:

a. The growing recognition of the importance of careers and educational guidance, particularly as a continuous process.
b. The increasing need for expertise in the staff-room as well as amongst officers of the careers service.
c. The problem of employment opportunities for older leavers with limited academic attainments.

As in the case of personal counselling, there is a wide range of opinion in Britain concerning the principles and practice of guidance. Some useful general guidelines were contained in a recent report by the Department of Education and Science.*

Careers Education in Secondary Schools, Education Survey 18, Department of Education and Science (HMSO, 1973).

The report suggested that an effective guidance process needs to have two stages: an *exploratory or divergent* stage, followed by a *convergent* one leading to decisions and choices concerning education and/or employment. Put more simply, this means that young people should first be encouraged to investigate all the various types of opportunities open to them, and then to narrow these down to a suitable choice in terms of their own aptitudes, interests and attainments.

How could this be achieved in practice? The *exploratory* stage, according to the DES report, can be catered for in a general way through the syllabus or by devoting some time on the timetable to careers and educational guidance. The point at which the *convergent* stage begins will vary according to the age at which pupils leave school or college. One important factor is the extent to which options have been kept open — through choice of subjects, degree of specialisation, and so on. It is fair to assume that upper-secondary or post-compulsory students have reached the stage where some degree of convergence must take place if it has not done so already. For at this point some educational and career choices — albeit provisional ones — have to be made.

Effective guidance at this stage requires systematic co-ordination and storage of information relating to individual students, and to employment and educational opportunities. According to the DES report, schools with a director of sixth form studies (or an equivalent) tend to be more successful in achieving this than schools without one. Co-ordination is of vital importance — without it, much of the advantage of having a guidance system is lost. One disturbing finding from the DES Inspectorate's survey was that:

Some schools, where careers education is rightly regarded as a team effort, reveal a lack of systematic consultation between tutors, subject teachers, the year heads and the careers team.

Shortage of time might be offered as a partial explanation, but it in no way excuses a total failure in this respect. Even so, it appears that relatively little time is devoted to careers and educational guidance in the majority of schools:

> ...only 15 per cent of all schools record that careers teaching occupies as much as one fifth of the work load of one member of staff. (DES survey — op. cit.)

THE CAREERS SERVICE AND SCHOOLS

If shortage of time is a problem for school-based guidance staff, it is also one for the hard-pressed officers of the Careers Service (formerly the Youth Employment Service). Criticism of existing guidance services has been prevalent for many years, and the Careers Service has borne the brunt of much of the attack, often simply because it has been an obvious target. Where schools and colleges provide little or no guidance themselves, it is easy to criticize those who are seen trying to provide information and advice.

The Careers Service is very much aware of its own shortcomings, handicapped as it is by a constant shortage of resources, including manpower. Its structure has always put the Careers Service at a disadvantage as far as personal contact with pupils is concerned. Often a careers officer's only meeting with a student consists of a brief interview shortly before he or she leaves school. So there is no opportunity for any kind of effective guidance to take place. Of course the problem would be *eased* if there were more careers officers with more time to devote to this aspect of their work; but it would not be *solved* while careers officers continued to be based outside schools and colleges and to have limited regular contact with them. Their position makes it virtually impossible for them to build up the detailed picture of individual students' interests, aptitudes, attainments and aspirations needed for effective guidance.

Perhaps it was for this reason that the 1971 report by the National Youth Employment Council* welcomed the 'substantial increase in interest in careers work in the schools and substantial progress in the schools' contribution to the process of vocational guidance'.

Certainly a great responsibility for guidance work lies with school- and college-based staff. They are often handicapped by a lack of contacts with and experience of the outside world of employers and employment: yet they do possess the great — and much-needed — advantage of being in a position to get to know the students.

Many of the schools and colleges which took part in our own research had — in conjunction with their tutor-counsellor system — assigned specific guidance duties to a small group of teachers. These worked, or tried to work, as a team despite the problem of co-ordination referred to earlier. Usually each member had a particular area of responsibility, such as university entrance, other educational opportunities, employment, and so on. In some schools and colleges, these members of staff had a lighter teaching timetable to allow them extra time to keep up-to-date with new information, to arrange activities linked with their guidance work and to attend meetings and conferences of special interest and relevance. Students in some of the

The Work of the Youth Employment Service 1968-1971, A Report by the National Youth Employment Council (HMSO, 1971).

schools and colleges were referred to guidance staff by their tutor-counsellor; in others they went directly to the guidance teacher concerned with their particular query or problem.

As in the case of tutor-counsellors, guidance staff were often anxious about their lack of time, accommodation and training. Those whose responsibility it was to provide information and advice on employment opportunities found this a special problem, particularly with regard to their limited experience of and contacts with the world of work. To a lesser extent, similar difficulties confronted teachers concerned with the provision of guidance on educational opportunities outside university or college of education. Many guidance staff also felt that they were as yet ill-equipped to inform and advise upper-secondary students with few or no formal qualifications, since this was a new situation which posed fresh problems.

THE PROBLEM OF THE 'UNQUALIFIED' 18-YEAR-OLD

The problems faced by older school leavers with modest (or non-existent) academic attainments have already been mentioned. In recent years they have caused concern amongst careers officers — a fact reflected in the 1971 report of the National Youth Employment Council, op. cit. The report explained that, in the past, industry was able to find potential 'material' for training as technicians and executives amongst its 16-year-old entrants. Recently more of these young people have chosen to remain longer in full-time education.

Faced with recruitment difficulties, some employers have adjusted their policy and training structure in order to take advantage of the increased supply of 17 and 18 year old leavers; other employers have not, and so have created difficulties not only for themselves but also for the school leavers concerned. The National Youth Employment Council therefore agreed that careers officers should encourage employers to consider recruiting and training these older leavers without A-Levels for technician and junior executive level jobs.

This is not a problem confined to Britain, of course. Both the 'unqualified' 18-year-old and the almost complete absence of industrially or commercially trainable youth at the age of 15 or 16 were mentioned as problems in Japan in the early 1960s, when more than 70 per cent were already staying on beyond the age of compulsory attendance (15). That country's experience, and similar problems in West European countries with an increasing staying-on rate would repay attention.

There is one other aspect which might be overlooked. The 18-year-old leaver apparently well qualified *for something* with two or three A-Levels may not be equipped either personally or academically for present forms of training or practical study at the end of the first post-compulsory phase, because of unwise study choices about the age of 16 or earlier. Readjustment of training schemes may indeed be called for; but a more obvious need is well informed career guidance earlier. The problem is clear enough in Britain; but some countries (like Germany) have recently felt it worse because of the late age of leaving school with a perhaps 'useless' *Abitur* or *baccalauréat*. (Indeed, Sweden has had the problem in acute form after university graduation.) The case for effective guidance on career and study prospects is thus reinforced. So is the case for 'recycling' opportunities at about the post-compulsory level of provision.

THE 'HINGE OF HISTORY'

In this chapter's examples the details of reorganisation matter little. The essential is *reorientation.* In *Only One World* Barbara Ward and René Dubois evoke a striking image when, describing the imbalance between the 'biosphere' of human inheritance and the 'technosphere' of man's creation, 'potentially in deep conflict', they say: 'And man is in the middle. This is the hinge of history at which we stand'.

School systems and their often tight social and economic links are part of an apparatus contrived mainly since the Industrial Revolution (in any sense that we know schools). They have no inherent justification *per se.* Without them, modern civilisation and social freedoms would be impossible; but their structures and working systems have already been overwhelmed by numbers, new demands, and the new instrumentation of learning and living — especially at the young adult phase. Not surprisingly, in all countries like our own (from which only a few typical examples have been drawn) comparable anxieties and dissatisfactions point to similar solutions — similar not in detail, but in intent.

Our 'hinge of history' is an educational renaissance. We are moving away from the superstition that the origin and ends of mankind's educational development are settled essentially, with only questions of local adaptation to be worked out. We are moving towards the realisation that a change of principle is upon us. In a quite altered technological, social, and political idiom the young adults of today are working together with us as full participants in shaping education for tasks previously beyond its imagination or powers. The essential newness of that concept and commitment marks our renaissance and its strategy.

The next chapter will be devoted to taking our bearings from the evidence now available.

4

SIGNPOSTS FOR
THE WAY AHEAD

Valuable indications for policy are already emerging from the trends and experiments discussed in previous chapters. The most important is the recognition of a new field of action, with a new style and new partnerships. Significantly, no familiar word previously described it; and most terms drawn from current use (like 'young adult') have been given a new connotation – perhaps a paradoxical one – in being applied to students above the age of 16 (still generally called 'pupils' in most European languages).

The adoption of the term 'post-compulsory' for the 16-20 age-group, perhaps including reference to slightly older students who are not in higher education, therefore invites justification. It is admittedly a less precise description than 'upper-secondary/lower-tertiary' as applied to schools and colleges; but it does focus attention on a new set of common features in a range of educational activities now considered generically for the first time. At least the description does not tie new concepts and modes to inherited institutions and practices which were not designed for them.

'Post-compulsory' may be criticised as too open-ended a term; yet perhaps there is no harm in that. Even the earliest post-compulsory education should be recognised as, in some sense, open-ended, though it may be rounded off temporarily at the age of 18, 21, or later with a certificate or other qualification. For that, in the nature of modern learning and working is always in some respects a provisional qualification. If the convention is accepted of calling the earliest post-compulsory years by that name to distinguish a particular threshold of attitudes, attainments, and choices, then it becomes simpler to use terms like 'higher' or 'vocational' or 'recurrent' education more precisely in their own right, and to recognise various styles of preparing for them (or just for life) in the post-compulsory learning of the youngest adults.

THE UNIVERSALITY OF NEWNESS IN POST-COMPULSORY EDUCATION

That is our significant point of departure. We began (as the Introduction shows) by looking for particular details of 'newness' — in the dimensions and composition of the enrolled population, in its unfamiliar elements and interests, in needs and job perspectives not previously represented, and in all the experimental responses made by those who provide education at this level.

Of course we continued to look for and analyse these things; but our central point of reference became the recognition that *all the students are new in vitally important ways,* and that the distinguishable elements of their newness very often reflect not just casual novelty but an *essentially new educational situation.* That may indeed mark the emergence of a differently ordered society; it certainly inaugurates a different structure of learning.

We found, too, that in discussing the educational and social 'crisis points' with colleagues from many types of

school or college for this age-group right across the world
there are comparable features of newness everywhere, and
important common factors to guide educational policy for
the post-compulsory level. What most clearly emerges is the
need for *a different approach to learning and teaching* —
beginning in compulsory schools, most marked at the level of
the young adult, but by implication relevant to every
prospect of later education and training.

At this point a personal explanation of attitude seems
called for. We did not set out with partisan views aligning us
somehow with 'youth', or causing us to see the classroom
(like some contemporaries) as a natural arena for conflicts of
culture and ideology. We have not arrived at that position.
From the beginning we tried to see factually in what ways
different aspects of newness were recognised by the teachers
and students themselves, what modifications of existing
institutions or programmes were recognised as helpful by the
participants, what alternative arrangements seemed
preferable, and what the significance of this information was
for policy and further enquiry. At that stage we were looking
for greater educational 'effectiveness' in the sense discussed
earlier (not didactic 'efficiency'), but within a familiar
framework. We felt special concern for the consequences of
larger enrolments, a wider social recruitment, or reforms of
structure, curriculum, and method lower down the school.
But our work 'on the ground', in the 'participant' kind of
research which was developed to give us the 'inside view'
required, left an intense conviction of the urgent need to
re-think in new terms the whole teaching/learning/research
relationship at the 'young adult' level in the post-compulsory
phase of education.

That reorientation does not abandon time-honoured
principles. It extends their applicability. In much the same
way, giving educational opportunity to women, to the 'lower

orders' and foreign subjects, or to the study of the sciences and technology, once represented a revolutionary turnabout. The present change called for may be further-reaching in its implications. Though the reorientation is largely school- or college-based in the first instance, and requires the partnership of *all* whose activities are so based, its repercussions throughout the whole of society and working life are such that they amount to a kind of educational renaissance. By that is meant an awakening to the educational possibilities and needs of transformed technological/social relationships. These obviously revolutionise learning and communications throughout life and work right across the world.

EXTENDING THE CONTEXT OF EDUCATIONAL RELEVANCE

Many alert young people and many of their teachers and observers are aware of these changes which are already upon us. A much greater number of students, without positive awareness, show uneasiness with their present situation and prospects in views very divergent from their teachers'. They show it in wanting 'a fresh start', in wishing they could have done something else, in dropping out altogether, in shocking the conventions, in 'unruliness', in criminality.

'Alienation' is an over-worked and emotionally coloured word. Let us think rather of 'unruliness'. In his 1974 Reith Lectures, Ralf Dahrendorf spoke of 'the restoration of governability' to public life. The main prerequisites he discerned (in addition to a strong Parliament with elected representatives in full control of government) were a full and responsible flow of information through the media (in all directions), and the establishment of intermediate levels of participant government and contributory expertise to build up 'governability', involving everyone. The need for a similarly cumulative partnership in all educational processes showed up strongly in all our research findings.

Professor Dahrendorf went on to specify some structural reorganisation of higher education programmes. The essential point here is to recognise the educational implications of what Dahrendorf said for all adults (including those just over 16). The educational future must be characterised by a full and responsible flow of learning opportunity throughout all living and working, with largely self-directed learning, strengthened by contributory participation in its intermediate 'management' and long-term development. That is a formula accepted generally for some professions (like teaching, in principle). The new technology of a 'communications society' and the awakening of demand for contributory relevance make it immediately applicable to young adult students too within the limits of their readiness and of local feasibility.

With special reference to post-compulsory education we strongly agree that courses of study (instead of being regarded as producers of 'spare parts' for industry and the professions) should, wherever possible, be broad and open, undertaken *per se* and personalising, and 'above all, *short*'. That last remark does not imply curtailment of education but 'worth-whileness' for the present. Post-compulsory education, in conferring adequate understanding and skill, is recognised as only *provisionally* sufficient since it is only the first stage of a lifelong process of self-development.

We focus Professor Dahrendorf's wider observations more narrowly on the post-compulsory phase of education for several reasons. That phase seems not only to us but to its members to be *a new beginning*. Beyond obligatory schooling which enrols everyone and is increasingly considered to be a broad, common basis, the 'young adult' phase opens up varieties of independent choice of study and life-style. It resumes study for many, and gathers in work- and life-experience for everyone. Those who 'never knew they had it in them', or 'never knew they could study and be trained for such things', or who simply never knew much about life at all during juvenile schooling, now embark upon their *adult education* formally as they do informally during leisure.

For the same set of reasons, governments everywhere, national commissions, and international agencies are beginning to look at the post-compulsory period of education with a fresh gaze. Some have bestirred themselves to positive action; but the time is short. In talking of 'governability' generally (but with an eye on education) Professor Dahrendorf warned of an impending flashpoint 'in two years' (from 1974). Many informed French observers expect 'another May 1968', as we saw. Whether overt student rebellion will occur anywhere, it is not for us to guess; but the signs of deep disaffection are widespread. Perhaps a greater cause for disquiet among policy-makers should be that such malaise pervades so many privileged students already selected for educational and career preferment in countries whose school/college systems have not yet really begun to cater for 'the others' on the doorstep, if not already unhappy inside. The long-term prospect is dismaying, unless a rapid change of perspective takes place. That is the context of today's decisions, and the forum for our research conclusions.

THE PERMANENCE OF CHANGE

We do not realise clearly enough that the state of impermanence to which many of our juniors are already adapting themselves is still more marked in the rapidly developing parts of the world. Change is faster not only in technologically advanced countries like the rest of the English-speaking world and Japan but in many low-income countries too. Most of our educational assumptions are still linked with expectations of some permanence, especially as they are exemplified in selection and grooming procedures for the highest academic positions which in turn push their influence back down the schools. Yet even in the countries longest industrialised and urbanised, school and higher education systems have developed their present form in less than two lifetimes (i.e., since the expansion of railways), and have been changing throughout that period.

The slow and very partial evolution of education in countries like those of Western Europe could not be a model for the USA after 1862, Japan after 1868, the USSR after 1917, or for the great rush of educational and political transformation after 1945 — even if institutions, techniques, and assumptions did continue for a while to repeat themselves. The expectations and attitudes were already different in these newer ventures. On a much more massive scale, and far faster-changing, the alteration in education's present and future potentiality perceived by alert young adults matches their appreciation of satellite communications or computer-aided storage and retrieval of information. Many of them already see the world and its knowledge as one system undergoing total readaptation.

Young adults are already *in* the world of the most advanced learning (at least in part) by means of television and other instrumentation. They are vital parts of commerce and its solicitations. They do not accept many of the controls to which they were once subject – any more than the Africans and the sheikhs. They are needed in greater numbers and variety than ever before – not in our present idiom, but in the increasingly experimental relationships with each other and with learning which *they* will work out over the years. We must come to terms with them for the sake of learning itself.

CONCEPTUAL IMPLICATIONS OF LIVING WITH CHANGE

It has always been believed that university teachers should be lifelong students, learning in fellowship. The legendary wandering scholar knew no boundaries, spoke a universal language, and feared no one if the Lord's enlightenment was on his side. Today, many of the young are in that case; though their lords of enlightenment are legion, the young mostly believe they have direct and universal access without the intermediacy of the scholastic priesthood or its particular formularies. That is what justifies talk of a renaissance or even a 'Reformation' atmosphere – especially when not even the learned now believe in much canonical knowledge, and most are aware that whole fields of knowledge change constantly beyond their ken.

Knowledge as such, in any objective sense, is not so penetratingly affected by present changes as the larger fields of humane awareness. It is true that entire fields of positive knowledge are new, and that old as well as new fields of knowledge are enlarging unpredictably. Of greater importance is the expansion and deepening of *subjective awareness* in the educational field, especially where young adults are concerned. We (and they still more, perhaps) are increasingly aware of *new aims* achievable not only *in* but *through* education. Young adults are confident of man's *power* to achieve them through technological and political activity. They often feel a positive obligation or *duty* to try to achieve improvements, especially by acting in concert with others. That is to say, they are sensitive to the moral and civic dimensions of educational reorientation. They expect us to make provision for these aspects within education; or, if they have despaired of us, they insist on handling them independently.

Our research showed repeatedly that the familiar plea for 'relevance' included not only job-utility, modernisation, and the like but sensitivity to the aspects just mentioned, which are essential for any civilisation. Many school programmes leave them out of account. Other curricula acknowledge their importance in theory or practice, but mostly in a didactic or 'initiating' way. That 'initiation' is often, too, into norms which modern men and women care little for – like those of team games and compliant 'law and order'. Intelligent learners at this age look instead for expressions of responsibility in action, participation in the 'management' of learning of every kind, and creative initiative. A change in this direction implies not simply a change of teaching/learning method, but the pursuit of different educational objectives. Those dimensions of personality long neglected in most school systems, or mainly left to extracurricular activities, are now at the very centre of young adults' aspirations in education – and of our aspirations for them.

Let us return to the question of access to knowledge, and its better distribution. In many parts of the educational world, lonely pioneers are still 'struggling to invent the wheel' (as one commentator put it). An immense amount of knowledge is not simply undistributed or unavailable; its very existence is unsuspected. The possibility of its relevance is unperceived even as a contingency. We see the problem easily enough when we consider the neglect of science, commerce, or even physical education and the education of girls, in school systems not far away in time or space. Yet most learned commentators observing educational systems now under challenge (like Janne, Géminard, Peterson and others already mentioned) agree with discontented young adults that whole realms of knowledge and experience have so far not sufficiently concerned the teachers and providers of upper-secondary education. These criticisms challenge especially the people concerned with the less traditional population and curriculum in the post-compulsory phase.

A huge awakening is an urgent imperative, with all the dispersal and application of new (or newly relevant) knowledge that that implies. Conversely, the recruitment of new and sometimes unsuspected skills is called for, to be cultivated by new means in circumstances far beyond those envisaged when nearly all school and college systems were being developed. Our research programme and contemporary books and papers have indicated important areas of new knowledge to be learned; but they all recognise too that some kinds of publicly needed knowledge are unknowable in any full sense — not just because objective knowledge is growing so fast but because subjective, 'participant' knowledge is required. That *experiential dimension* has seemed important to us not merely as a learning aid but as *continuously contributing* something essentially fresh and necessary to humane understanding. It is particularly relevant in the frontier area of the over-16s.

EDUCATIVE EXPERIENCE AND PARTICIPATION

Many formerly rigid barriers between schools and parents, or between school/college and work, are already breaking down − not everywhere, indeed, but significantly. This trend is noticeable in countries of every political complexion: in the USSR, the USA, and Denmark, and to a much smaller extent in Britain. In recent years that trend towards 'participation' has become a definite policy − of the central government in Sweden, of some local education authorities in Britain, and of organisations like the Confederation for the Advancement of State Education (CASE). In Britain many teachers fear or even resent such participation; in Japan the powerful teachers' union is strongly in favour. There is no doubt we shall see more of it.

On the higher education level, especially since the early 1960s, free use has been made of 'sandwich' organisation of courses, alternating work experience with study in college. The huge growth of degree courses under the auspices of the Council for National Academic Awards (CNAA) has not merely incorporated this principle generally but has actually related undergraduate studies ever more closely to specific career objectives, and local or regional enterprise. That injection of realism is felt by many to be an enhancement of the academic content rather than otherwise. One great advantage is that work and study are integrated, instead of both suffering the attrition previously experienced when so many occupation-linked studies were conducted on a part-time basis.

Lower down the scale, the Ordinary National Certificate (ONC) offering one day a week in college (in highly specific vocational or pre-professional preparation) has been eclipsed in many students' and colleges' ambitions by the Ordinary National Diploma (OND), which is awarded for full-time studies. In our sample, students preparing for the OND were hard working and enthusiastic for their specific objective, if not perhaps blinkered by it. But that is not surprising, for several reasons: the course-work is narrowly prescribed; the students need minimum qualifications to begin it; the diploma and the job often appear to be the sole (rather than the immediate) aim of the course; and if any further qualification is envisaged it is usually an intensification of the same thing, at HND level or in a degree. Of course, colleges encourage students to participate in social or generally cultural activities; but these hardly ever seem germane to the training given in courses. It must be said that the remarks in this paragraph apply to all continental institutions and courses of the same general type — if not more so.

Yet industry and commerce call out for resourceful flexibility. The structural evolution of all enterprises, the extension of technological ingenuity, and everyone's growing concern for civilised social contacts all demand more 'professional' *education* rather than trained techniques. Students in technical training often see themselves as educational paupers (as is well shown in G. Vincent, op. cit., and M. Aumont, *Jeunes dans un monde nouveau* (1974)). To redress this narrowness and abject status many expedients have been tried, of which some have been mentioned already: including technical studies within the framework of university-admission examinations; turning techniques into technologies either verbally or actually; broadening the base of study by inserting 'cultural' elements which are seldom appreciated; and requiring all students to take some common courses.

Such stratagems all have their advocates; but they may miss the point because of two hang-overs from school. First, the emphasis is still on *instruction,* whereas we know that for *educational effectiveness* some things have to be *learned* (like morality, music and true love). Secondly, the assumption is that all the teaching/learning must be done during some *initial* phase wherein people are stuffed with the essentials. If only we accept the prospect of periodicity, and follow the initial period of post-compulsory education with 'recycling', 'recurrent education' and the like, the first pressure can be eased and narrow specificity can be broadened.

Organisationally, this aim is made easier by the wide acceptance of 'units', 'modular learning', 'credits', and so forth. Though these are still only just beginning to be familiar in higher education, that does not prevent their adoption in post-compulsory education. The point is more obvious when we recall that a 'young adult' college is already in some ways or for some people the earliest example of 'short-cycle higher education'.

Acceptance of this concept generally makes it easier to take some pressure off schools' curricula lower down the age-range, too. Without loss of zest and quality, the sheer material content of much instruction could be lightened to take account of new fields of interest and human values, as well as hitherto neglected but now necessary skills. Much necessary content is quickly mastered when adult commitment replaces juvenile drill. 'Young adult' colleges can not work miracles; but their special kind of atmosphere, with the future clearly opening ahead, has impressed most who have had experience of them.

In the British context it seems important to point to moves by the Schools Council (in 1974) towards the introduction of courses on industry 'into schools'. The Confederation of British Industry and the Trades Union Congress both welcomed the initiative, which was also blessed by officials of the National Union of Teachers. About the same time, the CNAA (most of whose degree courses have a strong practical orientation) welcomed moves towards broadening 'sixth form studies'. That description obviously subsumes similar work in colleges. Yet in all these proposed expedients there are limits on what can be expected from teaching *about* industry, management, and the like. We need to know more about the possibilities of *experiential* learning — not as it has been tried hitherto, but as enlightened in new approaches to the education of young adults.

EXPANDING AWARENESS AND COMBINING PERCEPTIONS

Awareness of important changes of attitude and concept in education is slow to percolate. The specialisation of administration, of school types, and of curricular patterns serves well recognised needs; but it may ossify what should be a living process of growth and adaptation. Relevant information may be ignored, may be unwelcome. Even information systems and disseminating agencies work within categories defined for needs different from those which now concern us. Some, like OECD and the National Foundation for Educational Research now face the challenge by feeding out pre-sorted .information (sometimes in the form of abstracts or working papers) to strategic points. Yet in the nature of things, 'education in the post-compulsory phase' is for most establishments a no man's land. Perhaps worse, it is claimed as so many small fiefs by warring establishments.

Therefore an important conceptual change is made when education between 16 and about 20 is recognised as a truly distinctive area of cumulative knowledge and expertise — in much the same way as pre-school education. Important in its own right, and perplexing still for lack of effective study, it is nevertheless pivotal to many decisions elsewhere in education because it is a threshold area where futures can be made or marred, and where past mischances can be corrected. At the time of writing, the NFER was preparing critical reviews of all research relevant to the over-16s (along with pre-school and remedial education). We welcome that British initiative (which our previous publication pleaded for).

At least the auguries are good. Both the Schools Council and the NFER now clearly recognise that 'expert' enquiries are not enough, even from the viewpoint of knowledge. Educational research is already moving towards much greater participation by the people on the ground. It seems obvious in British circumstances that teachers should be active and responsible members of all such research and development activity. The strength of teacher representation on the Schools Council and the spread of teachers' centres show how much we take teacher participation for granted in educational innovation. But why should that partnership stop at teachers? The Schools Council itself (1964) is little more than ten years old; and in some countries (even in our survey) no one yet involves the teachers in rethinking education or enquiring into its problems. Carefully gathering — indeed, incorporating — the experience and views of all others alert to education's new perspectives is not much more revolutionary than placing so much responsibility on British teachers' shoulders.

Teachers are often rightly annoyed if someone without school experience tells them what to do. Yet teachers and educational 'managers' of every kind are often guilty of a similar fault in prescribing externally for young adults. Certainly they know the parameters and administrative constraints limiting some kinds of educational aspiration, usually in a material sense. But they have *never* really been inside the world in which young adult students now live, since the world remembered from their youth (especially the school/college world of the over-16s) was different not only in its dimensions and outer contacts but in its inner experience and concepts. Even teaching experience gives only one side of the picture. Therefore discussions on the development of existing educational systems, and still more enquiries into their potential future, require the inclusion of the 'inside view' of the senior students at least – and also of those directly concerned with them in 'the real world' beyond the school walls.

This is no utopian prescription. Student representation already exists – though not often at the 16-plus level in Britain, except in colleges of further education and some junior or sixth form colleges which have adopted their style. Where school or college councils are established, these seldom have powers of positive recommendation on any matters of serious educational importance. In any case, 'representation' does not get to the heart of the matter. What we need is communication, with permeation of ideas. It seems much more important to secure young adults' views on education (their own educational future) than to have them voting in trade union and works council activities, since we are considering not *ad hoc* operational decisions but the building up of insights from many quarters. For the same reasons, the inclusion of insights from other interested parties is vital; and it should be ensured continuously. The much-quoted 'rolling reform' process in Sweden is an example which does not come amiss. Though far from perfect, the activities of the National Board of Education (which is *not* the Swedish Ministry of Education) would repay open-minded study.

It is, of course, important to heed research and the expert's scholarship; but the permanence of change and the supreme importance of *informed judgement* (rather than insensitive 'prediction') nowadays take much educational decision-making out of the realm of computation and into areas of subtle perception or preference. The quantified evidence and well-slotted categories which served educational policies so deftly in the 1940s and 1950s are now brought into question by our better understanding of education as largely a social process in which personal involvement and 'internalised' learning replace the image of an efficient machine. In any case, technical exactness and computerised facts are not the only things we are after by any means; they might produce no more than a sort of historical snapshot — sharply defined, interesting, and perhaps useful; but not after the crisis of decision has moved on.

Accepting the importance of constantly evolving perceptions, therefore, implies quite altered relationships in all processes of research, development, and implementation — not least in 'frontier' schools and colleges like those engaging the activities of the over-16s. Most of all, perhaps, there are profound implications for teachers' roles, with consequential implications for the training and in-service development of teachers for this age-range.

TEACHERS AND YOUNG ADULTS: AN EXPLORATION IN COMMON

At several points in this book the present and future roles of teachers in relation to young adult full-time students have been touched on, rather than considered. No general statement can be validly made about teachers' present position with regard to the over-16s, since teachers come from almost every conceivable academic background. They are now employed teaching over-16s in grammar schools, comprehensive schools, technical colleges, sixth form colleges and even (in some countries) teacher-training colleges — all at the 'upper-secondary' level treated in this book. They are in selective and open-admission institutions, coeducational and single-sex. Their professional attitudes range from the obstinate isolationism of the *Philologenverband* and the *Société des Agrégés* to remarkable harmony and friendship with their students.

But no teacher is quite 'ready for the over-16s' — or could be, because what we are talking of (more than at any other point of education) is the start of a voyage of exploration on which young adults will continue long after their teachers are left behind. In any case, the factual evidence and central hypotheses of post-compulsory education are only now being presented to teachers in the full relevance that takes them beyond familiar local problems. That is why the Department of Education and Science during the past few years has arranged so many 'workshops' and conferences on 'Education, 16-19', drawing together teachers, principals, and advisors from every type of establishment. Similar conferences have been arranged for inspectors (whose work in Britain is almost entirely advisory). The Further Education Staff College at Coombe Lodge and a number of other establishments throughout the country are engaged from time to time on the same problems. The Council of Europe's sponsorship of similar study meetings was mentioned earlier.

Yet these very welcome enterprises have several shortcomings in common. They are occasional. Their starting-base is the present array of institutions, practices, and qualifications. In old-fashioned language, it is sometimes hard to see the wood for the trees. The revealing 'new view', the hypothesis which will be a catalyst for action desired and necessary, eludes most participants. Even if that were not so, where are the teachers and services to carry on the good work that innovators might propose?

Several necessities are evident. There is no point in having so many people looking at 'sixteen plus' and seeing so many different animals. There is little point, either, in converging for the time of a conference and then going back to starting point. The developing needs of young adults' education in the immediately post-compulsory phase are recognisable enough – but hardly ever 'at one go' to any single person or group. Therefore the apparatus must be established to collect all the perceptions and recommendations, and to bring them as required to the point of critical discussion – always with a view to experimental implementation and continuous feedback.

In the first instance, it may be supposed, that kind of information and the new perspectives will be brought to young teachers in initial training *specifically for this age-group.* Yet in-service development and reorientation are equally vital. This kind of self-guidance and mutual counselling obviously brings in the necessary contact with guidance and counselling personnel, together with those specialising in some problems of young adults. (So the McNair Report recommended for teacher training generally as long ago as 1944.)

In the entire reorientation required for dealing with this new educational entity, our own research programme showed how ready many teachers and entire schools were to share in discussions of our findings and those of others. That brings us to a pivotal point in deciding what may be done to help teachers. As we noted before, teachers especially resent advice or imposition of programmes if presented 'from above' or 'by outsiders'. Participant enquiry about present turmoil in the upper-secondary schools, and participant discussion of essential problems and possible solutions, must engage the goodwill and experience of teachers actually involved – and the students themselves. Yet that is not enough.

The generic view of the whole, and the constant updating

necessary, must obviously come from nationally concerted action, supported by the kind of research report we offer. Universities and research centres will be focal points of enquiry and communication; but 'research and development' centres with strong connections in the centres of experience and experiment themselves are integral to successful pioneering in this frontier area.

Someone must begin specifically somewhere. At King's College in the University of London, postgraduate students preparing to teach can follow a 'curriculum option' course on 'Education 16-20' in the perspective recommended in this book. A post-experience M.Ed. course on the same theme has been approved. Other universities and colleges are beginning to develop similar opportunities. But a nexus of all similar enterprises is necessary, preferably on a national scale.

In the long run, however, success in preparing teachers for (or in) post-compulsory education depends on cumulative research and development enterprise not only in universities and similar centres, or in government departments, but in the schools and colleges where young adults and their own teachers embark together on this exciting voyage of new learning. In the nature of young adults' present contacts, that exploration is international.

5

CONCLUSIONS AND
RECOMMENDATIONS

The previous chapter gathered together, from our own and others' evidence, the essential features of post-compulsory education as we see them. By implication we highlighted guidelines for policy. In the present chapter we set forward some practical conclusions and recommendations for the way ahead.

Of course we have ideas of our own about education beyond the scope of the investigation we undertook together; but the recommendations offered here arise directly out of our research itself or from collateral studies undertaken in connection with it. Previous ideas and experience were greatly affected by the impact of our study of the 16-20 age-group at this critical time.

Our recommendations and other observations in this chapter fall into three main sections: those concerned with institutional provision and reorientation; observations on counselling and guidance; and observations on curriculum, teaching/learning arrangements, and personal relationships within establishments for the 16-20 age-group.

The last-mentioned limitation illustrates a point of fundamental importance for us. We do not set ourselves up as curriculum experts, for example. We have studied the post-compulsory age-range with the help of its teachers, students, and researchers in our own and other countries. What we have to say relates to that field of interest, seen generically and from inside as far as possible, though in a perspective of comparative analysis and long-term development. Our recommendations apply in the first instance to the 16-20 age-range (or comparable levels of attainment); and if we stray beyond that it is because we think that the 'young adult' phase of learning today carries implications for earlier or later education. We always come back to 'newness' in post-compulsory education — 'total newness', we might say — as our point of reference.

INSTITUTIONAL REORIENTATION AND POLICY DEVELOPMENT

Earlier chapters spelt out some details of that generic newness. Here we are trying to hold on to certain constants in our recommendations. We focus our thoughts about decisions and programming primarily on Britain, with a view to helping policy and development in a practical way; but we hope the general validity of our advice may help colleagues abroad who have thought over post-compulsory education's problems with us, and provided such a wealth of evidence. Certain problems remain constantly with us. Among these are questions of access to learning, student 'flow', permeability of institutions and courses, and the development of options within and after post-compulsory education. We shall look at some of these problem areas, making recommendations or observations, before offering general recommendations for the reorganisation of post-compulsory provision.

The Question of Staying on

For administrators the first problem is where and how to accommodate the students, and to know (if possible) how many they will be and of what types. Though their most recognisable features may differ, they have much in common. In any case, increasingly 'polyvalent' provision will serve many of their varied needs. So the question of variety may be less pressingly important for administrators and planners than the numbers likely to be involved.

How many will there be? Though there may be more hesitation about staying on immediately after 16, there are very strong indications that the post-compulsory population will continue to expand over a long period. In the short term, perhaps, there will be a 'stutter' in enrolment increase; and fears of eventual unemployment or other topical factors may influence potential students' readiness to come forward. But periods of recession are usually periods of *more* (not less) enrolment in education likely to enhance employability: and we are also talking about countries like Britain where the percentage enrolled in post-compulsory education is still modest by world standards. Therefore it is advisable to count on much more staying on, and the need to provide for it, either immediately after the end of compulsory school or after a period of working experience. Besides, there are many areas of the country and some groups (girls, for example) who have not yet taken full advantage of their opportunity.

On the other hand, it seems likely that students will more carefully weigh possible advantages and disadvantages in post-compulsory education. There will probably be less unreflecting staying-on for its own sake or for social reasons. By the same token, students will doubtless be more selective in the opportunities they choose, if they are well informed about them. There will very likely be less willingness to think of either post-compulsory education or higher education as the inevitable (or only justifiable) consequence of what has gone before. Students will therefore be less content to accept whatever just happens to be available. They are already more mobile and adaptable than their predecessors; and they are more 'choosy'. Unfortunately, their choices are often haphazard and in the long run not always very helpful to themselves. No system could simply become a supermarket for consumers of education. Effective counselling and guidance services working in close co-operation with the providers and planners of post-compulsory education are essential both to potential students and to the development of the system.

Possible trade recession is no argument for contraction. That would be suicidal in the present state of international competition, which will become more intense. Misgivings about choice and quality are right and proper. The appropriate reaction is not, however, to freeze off the opportunity (which would do no good either to the students or to the country) but to make it effective. The underprivileged groups of people who do not yet have their fair share of even imperfect educational opportunity would come off worst in any policy of contraction.

Effective counselling and guidance services, combined with existing facilities for tutorial care in schools and colleges, will doubtless guard against unfortunate choices and passive staying-on. But how can deliberate and well-informed staying-on be more effective? Many students who actually succeed in obtaining important credentials (like A-Levels, the *baccalauréat* or the *Abitur*) are 'fit for nothing else' in the opinion of higher education officers and potential employers alike. A more serious criticism is that of young adults themselves, who at the end of the course sometimes wonder what it was all in aid of. A growing number certainly wonder if the next stage is going to be worth it. What seems an obvious move from the conventional school classroom may seem much less automatic or desirable from another type of upper-secondary establishment.

Widening the Range of Transition Points

Without prejudice to the prospects of those whose career might well be fulfilled by going on to familiar higher education, alternatives in that very field now raise serious questions. Most old assumptions about what constituted study 'at sixth form *level*' really blinkered attention to a *narrow range* of subjects. A sharp focus on the *prescribed syllabus* within those chosen subjects further obscured their wider possibilities for sheer interest or career use. The bulk of A-Level studies are in a quite restricted range of subjects, both nationally and in individual schools. In one academically successful school in our sample, which prides itself on the broad range of available subjects, and where over 90% of the students in the research programme were doing 3 or more A-Levels, almost 43% were taking those examinations entirely in mathematics and physics. Any wider national survey shows that students specialising on the science side relatively rarely include any 'humanities' or arts subject. Conversely, though the arts students quite often include a 'humanities' or social study, relatively few of them choose any scientific or applied study other than geography or economics. A 1973 total of 21.2% taking both arts and science subjects was hailed as a 'further increase'. Even within the range of choices, the variation is predominantly confined to the most familiar options.

So advocating the opportunity for a much wider range of choices is no prescription for anarchy, or for a do-it-yourself mixture with little future in jobs or higher education. It is much more a case of providing alternatives appealing to interest and practicality, and having a *prima facie* career prospect in further study or employment.

Upper-secondary schools' and colleges' links with higher education and industry will doubtless be strengthened as the years pass, through the expansion of linked and 'taster' courses, through interchange of personnel and services in consortia, and perhaps through growing acceptance at this level too of 'sandwich' and other cyclical arrangements already familiar in higher education. Undoubtedly, too, much more attention will be given to the possibilities of *part-time* post-compulsory education, since that has been included in British legislation for over 50 years and is quite familiar in other countries. (The chief snags shown up by experience have been: wear-and-tear on the students, followed by a heavy drop-out rate; 'irrelevant' content; and poor co-ordination between 'theory' and practical life experience.)

Colleges of 'Sixth Form' and 'Further Education' Types

To satisfy these multifarious but important requirements, administrators as well as students look more and more to further education colleges and 'sixth form' or junior colleges. Their popularity proves much more than their ability to provide instruction and/or training of the many types desired. It reflects satisfaction of a wider range of young adult needs in education as a whole. Without any doubt, some of the 'secondary' sixth form colleges already provide a 'young adult' atmosphere which is a great advance on the protective paternalism of most ordinary sixth forms even in relaxed schools; but, as compared with 'further education' the 'secondary' sixth form colleges face difficulties of both an administrative and an educational kind as soon as we count up the desiderata to which attention has been given here.

One of these is provision for 'returners'. Another is the need to provide short courses (one year or less) for a student body so far rather unfamiliar but claiming increasing attention. Provision must be made for:

a. Those called 'non-traditional sixth-formers' in the Schools Council Working Party Papers, who may often be rounding off previous studies or preparing themselves for such careers as nursing, child care, journalism, and so on which in Britain have *so far* not become graduate professions.

b. Those requiring some specific element to enable them to enter an important professional apprenticeship or an institution of higher education — which might consist of several associated studies or an intensive course in one.

c. 'Updating' courses on secondment, but not at the university level (where this type of provision is already accepted).

d. 'Conversion' courses to meet the requirements of structural change in occupations or the development of new professional activities.

Much of this kind of thing, hitherto with a strongly vocational orientation, has long been provided in colleges of further education; but the growing requirement of a broad general base of study for vocational/technical expertise now makes more of this work reach the *level* of 'sixth form studies' without resembling their structural pattern. Nevertheless, some overlapping provision (instruction in mathematics, some branches of science, languages and social studies, for example) could be encouraged with good results both educationally and socially. For these and similar reasons it seems probable that more administrators and policy-makers will be attracted to solutions of the Barnstaple or Preston type, whereby *all* the over-16 provision is based upon 'further education' premises. Or else they will encourage the collateral development of a similar enterprise in 'further education' alongside existing sixth forms or 'secondary sixth form colleges', though with ever stronger reliance on a consortium of co-ordinated services *and contacts.* Some promising consortium arrangements have been cheated of full success because not enough attention has been paid to the necessity for regarding all participating establishments as fully collegiate elements of one provision.

Towards a Better Use of Resources

Where school sixth forms continue to be a vigorous part of the local provision (as may well happen where they have a strong staff, good resources, and an aura of some sort) it is obvious that they cannot remain self-sufficient. No matter how well they may have done in the past, they have concerned themselves with only a part of what is now necessary – even at the level they so confidently regard as their own. For example, a large number of English sixth forms are still not coeducational – an anachronism, indeed, as the clustering of mixed groups of students at the end of any school day shows.

Desperately needed resources, including personnel, are too often locked away or used by a few students during a short day, instead of being opened up for more general use. To some extent the principle is accepted that they should be available; for example, in evening institute work on the premises of some of them. But the whole system needs to be rethought structurally to benefit all post-compulsory students. That presupposes day-time availability to young adults too.

Schools, adult education, and further education divisions familiar in Britain falsify the logical interrelationships of many kinds of education at the level with which we are concerned. Clearly, the regulations must be altered. Long before that may happen, it is possible for administrators and education committee members to decide what use should be made of existing premises and facilities, and where financial and similar resources should be allocated. We unhesitatingly support the steady trend among local education authorities and the students themselves in favour of 'college' rather than 'school' for the over-16s; and we also foresee that 'college' will increasingly mean part of the 'further education' provision – either as a junior but integral part of an existing establishment, or as part of an F.E.-based consortium (very likely as an interim measure).

If and when circumstances permit the establishment of a 'community college' in the sense discussed earlier, but with more 'young adult' and far less 'schooly' characteristics than some aspirants to the title of 'community college' now possess, another important step will be taken. Less advanced (e.g., pre-A-Level) 'tertiary' provision in manifold variety could be widespread in new-style community colleges acting also as adult education centres. The material basis is often there already, especially if modern libraries and the like are counted in. The so far missing resource is the change of attitude which could switch local authority policy within the existing framework of legislation and expenditure.

On the other hand, local adaptation of existing resources has plagued Britain with a maze of 'ad-hockery' in which relevant information and rational purpose are lost. A shrewd educational observer has claimed that most educational policy development in England is determined by the use of *buildings.* In the nature of things, these durable objects were not intended to do what we now want; but brisk decisions can transform their use and opportunities. (Think of the old workhouse buildings still used in a transformed world!) The real framework for policy in post-compulsory education is that firm evidence of actual needs and practicable expedients which is now available, together with information and insights presented by interested persons *in the centres of experience,* not in the administrative blocks or ivory towers. Furthermore, the pivot of relevance is no longer in one country or one occasion. Relevance is international, research-linked, and complementary, relying on feedback from experiments in all similar circumstances.

Giving Post-Compulsory Education its own Organisation

It goes without saying, therefore, that one necessary reorganisation of structure is to recognise post-compulsory education as a distinct entity (of course), and to provide it with its own consultative organs, administrators, and teachers who will devote attention to it as a critically important *genre.* Already there are preparatory and in-service courses for teachers concerned with this age-group and attainment-level. That is welcome; but unless there is a career structure for teachers in post-compulsory education itself there is a risk that the Cinderella experience of adult education tutors, remedial specialists and the like will be repeated. What we are talking about is not the development of a supplementary provision with supplementary and part-time teachers but the preparation of a most significant sector of the teaching profession, with a tougher and more delicate job than academic school teachers or college lecturers as we know them today.

Post-compulsory education by reason of its present variety and intrinsic adaptability to the future requires dedicated study, resilient resourcefulness, teamwork and management skills on a scale beyond most present imagination. The excitement of being in on the beginning of an educational innovation has produced apostles and missionary zeal, with some spectacular success. These are perilous benefits, and ephemeral — especially if someone is promoted. Therefore the establishment of a cadre of effective teachers for post-compulsory education requires not simply a high level of personal quality, competence and drive in the teachers themselves but strong official backing to ensure support and continuity.

We see this backing requirement in two ways — structurally and operationally. The responsible organisation must be established to provide it, comprising not only a department for post-compulsory education at local authority and national levels but a network of specific connections for research and review. Some of these may represent the intermediate level of participant management and local oversight spoken of earlier. The whole enterprise at its various levels needs constant contact with those responsible for curriculum development and for the supply or modification of study aids and materials. For these the need is unprecedented; but the hidden risk is that commercial interests, unguided, may pre-empt the business of satisfying it in the obvious, older idiom. To provide real learning opportunities for this new world of education it is vital to engage the partnership and policy suggestions of all those already involved in the pioneering of post-compulsory education.

That of course includes the teachers. If these are to be good teachers, their norms of practice and evaluation will be strongly influenced by daily contact with students with whom they are in tune. That, however, means being linchpins of innovation, not Peter Pans. If effective personal interchange is to give rise to something more important, the feedback from teaching/learning must be effectively part of a real system of communications and joint management — not only within the establishment where they work. Indeed, if that itself is not to be blinkered, it needs the external challenge of others' experience and scholarship at all levels.

All this means seeing post-compulsory education within the changing dynamics of the entire system of education and the working life of the community. These cannot really be appreciated within the boundaries which often divide school thinking from considerations of daily life outside. Nor can they be understood without reference to experience in quite other kinds of learning and training. After all, that is the way in which young adults now apply criteria to their own lives.

Ideal and Interim Reorganisation

The clutter of institutions and practices which we have inherited is often said to give Britain more experimental possibilities than other countries. That is true; but we have also more chances to lose ourselves in a maze. Firms, trades unions, and all kinds of professional organisations are now regrouping themselves for more effective action in a world which their previous structure was unprepared for. Local and regional government is reorganised, mainly to continue the perennial purposes of peaceful and agreeable living, but with the new instrumentation and contacts required by modern technology.

Amidst all this reorganisation it would be unthinkable that

education (by its very nature foward-looking) should not change its sights and methods. Yet in many countries the 'education industry' (the biggest, the most expensive, and the most labour-intensive) is the worst organised of all. At least, it is the least reorganised for the needs of tomorrow. That criticism is far from original; but it must be repeated here because we are less concerned with whether it has done its old job well than with whether it can extend its commitments to provide services and opportunities previously uncalled for — perhaps not previously envisaged.

For that new conspectus of commitments an ideal situation might arise if all were equally convinced of what was necessary, and in the same way; or if people were starting *de novo,* as in a new town with new establishments and new staff and a group of students newly gathered together. Such new or nearly new situations do occur, but rarely. Occasionally the opportunity offers itself when a large new school or college has to be built for some other purpose. In such circumstances we unhesitatingly recommend the establishment of a community college — primarily for the 16-20 age-range (or equivalent attainment levels), but also giving older adults access to all the facilities spoken of here (counselling, guidance, information, and recreational and aesthetic opportunities). It is not our province to say how it should be officially administered; but one point of emphasis seems very important — that it should essentially be a centre of learning and reorientation for young adults (not for 'youth' or peripheral activities) opening up the continuum of adult and higher learning.

There are a few such centres already in Britain; and others might be established by modification of something existing now, such as a lively school or further education centre already adapted for adult and community use. The goodwill engendered where that happens makes us optimistic for the steady progress of this new tendency within limited financial resources, now restricted officially to the provision of 'roofs over heads' in schools or colleges. Yet a roof can cover many people and purposes by more extended use.

The scarcest resource is personnel; and the most expensive item in the educational budget is teachers' salaries. Many teachers at the upper-secondary or college level teach small groups, though redistribution of time and location could bring the opportunities they represent within reach of more (and more varied) students. Joint appointments for school, school/college, and 'further'/community combinations of service are not merely feasible but becoming familiar. All would gain thereby, including most of the teachers and many of their under-16 students as well as those above the age of compulsory attendance. Joint use of facilities and personnel in this way has been familiar for a generation in Denmark and the USA.

Besides, we are not thinking only of ordinary teachers. Unfortunate experience of the employment of traditional secondary school teachers in adult education, without very considerable reorientation, has caused many education authorities and advisors to decide against their use. We have recommended the training and development of a special teaching body for the post-compulsory phase; but as an alternative we obviously recognise two other sources. One is the group of teachers and trainers engaged in further education, who with moderate re-training and informed reorientation are perhaps more attuned to young adults' learning needs. Another is the well educated and professionally competent population in the neighbourhood who never thought of themselves as teachers in the conventional sense but whose goodwill can be tapped successfully, as experience already shows. Scientists, technologists, doctors, and people in the arts or other fields of public life are examples of potential teachers able to get on especially well with young adults. They are not, of course, the only source of supply; but neither are ordinary teachers.

The kind of provision envisaged brings us to the example afforded by several types of university extra-mural work and by the Open University, both of which have important attachments to local centres while drawing centrally upon the expertise and scholarship of bodies possessing resources far beyond those of schools or other local institutions. Close-circuit or longer-range broadcasting supplements, and all the apparatus of casettes, microfiches, and other information storage systems, can multiply and vastly extend the contacts of scarce personnel. What of personal contacts on the spot? Of course that is where they are required; but the very use of these wider information sources allows the teacher/tutor on the spot to be fully a 'resource *person*' instead of an expensive channel of knowledge. Many kinds of knowledge and insight desired (and half-possessed) by many young adults are beyond the competence of even a good, unaided teacher.

Young Adult Provision 'Without Walls'

The kinds of provision just discussed recall the 'University without walls' in the United States. Though that is not primarily (or even significantly) concerned with our age-group, it is often operating at the attainment-level we are contemplating. Similar remarks apply to the American community colleges. We Europeans have therefore much to learn from studying them with reference to the functional needs we are examining, and without being disturbed by differences of circumstance. The same note applies to some European continental alternatives which appear to be doing in another context the kinds of thing we wish to achieve in ours. Of these, one of the most important is to open up the school or college — internally to itself, beyond that to other learning-points in the neighbourhood, and further afield to advanced learning — whether in 'higher' education or in the world at large.

Therefore, while we look forward eventually to a 'community college' type of provision where that can be established, we welcome the widening establishment of 'junior colleges' either on their own or as parts of 'further education' provision. 'Sixth form colleges' within the secondary range are welcomed too; but for the reasons already given they seem bound to forgo certain proper expectations. Several prerequisites which seem to us essential are not always present. We believe that the colleges should offer open access, be co-educational, be polyvalent in serving the neighbourhood — especially for young adult 'returners', be prepared to cater for part-time study, and offer 'un-packaged' study programmes to suit individuals' personal profiles of attainment and interest. It goes without saying, too, that every establishment should co-operate closely with counselling and guidance services for older as well as younger adults. Since curricular features and counselling are examined separately in this chapter, we continue here with other structural aspects.

Easing the Process of Institutional Transition

As long as schools continue to be the main providers of 'sixth form' opportunities, certain practical problems of an administrative or structural kind must be faced. Apart from the existence of separate school/FE regulations (which could be merged at this level), there is the problem that teaching and other staff are usually appointed to one school in effect, though technically employees of the local education authority. They feel they belong to the school as a whole, and that it belongs to them. In referring to consortia we have already commented on the need to pool not merely resources but goodwill. Schools' departmental structure and some all-school activities already produce small and large staff teams with strong corporate feelings.

In order to make full use of these often advantageous features, reorganisation needs to be accompanied by close consultation and conversion if possible, though (since no school belongs to its staff) policy decisions need not wait on the latter. But as a matter of commonsense good staff teams and personal expertise do need to be held together wherever possible, so as to provide the nucleus of an intended junior college. The personal crises experienced in any structural rearrangement (even, for example, for a new syllabus) can be acute; but they are more intense if staff feel that 'their' school and the corporate reality to which they have devoted their lives will be 'abolished'. Structural rearrangement of institutions, programmes, and personnel therefore requires sensitive handling. At the same time, a dilly-dally policy does no good. The best solution seems to be a firm policy, with emphasis on the positive advantages *for all.* As we saw, the verdict of those who have experienced the move has been far more favourable than otherwise. As an essential preliminary during an interim period, the process of breaking down the walls gradually by institutional co-operation can have a markedly educative effect.

One important transition is so obvious that it is often overlooked — the transition from compulsory school to a sixth form or college of 'volunteer' students. At one time, entry into a small, privileged 'sixth' brought its own kind of ecstasy — for some, at least. The sense of being 'special' immediately and in prospects was a balm to any anxieties arising from the change in work-style; and there was often a significant corporate feeling too. Now, with more than half of the age-group staying on, much of that has gone, especially if people stay on in the same establishment.

Where there is change of establishment — as from a 'feeder' school to an enlarged sixth form or a college — the transition can be troublesome. The advantages of a fresh start in a new place are clear in many instances, and the 'young adult' atmosphere recalls the sense of privilege mentioned in the previous paragraph; but to get full benefit from its opportunities students need to be prepared for the transition lower down the school system. If a more independent style of work, and team-experience, can be initiated there, that is a great advantage.

Thus both teachers and their students need to be prepared well in advance for the important transition from compulsory to post-compulsory education. The need for good counsel and a full and sympathetic picture is obvious. That would have been true before the recent transformation of the post-compulsory scene; but it is essential for adequate preparation now. For these reasons the research programme paid a very great deal of attention to the amount and kind of advice or other assistance received by students before they entered the post-compulsory phase, as well as during it. Some of that evidence has been given earlier, when we discussed 'crisis' points, and also when we considered various types of provision already made at the upper-secondary level. Our conclusions from that survey, and recommendations, are given in the section which follows.

COUNSELLING AND GUIDANCE

What Students Expect from Counselling and Guidance

Our research showed that upper-secondary students had definite ideas about the kind of guidance they needed and wanted. The following requests were those most frequently made:

Table 4. English Students' Wants and Needs with Respect to Counselling and Guidance*

Type of provision	% of Students
Personalised guidance about employment opportunities	20
General information about the range of employment opportunities	16
General information about the nature of employment opportunities	13
Visits to places of work/ educational institutions	12
Personalised guidance on educational opportunities	11
Talks by people in various occupations	10

In their comments many students emphasised the *importance of a personal and individual approach to guidance:*

Staff cannot possibly be expected to know what type of person you

*Adapted from Table 51 in *Post-Compulsory Education I: A New Analysis in Western Europe* (1974), 352.

are and advise you as to the most advantageous subjects to take. How can they possibly be expected to guide people whom they have never met before?

More interest should be taken in the individual so that the staff are able to help more in advice on the suitability of a student for a certain job. Students should each have a regular time to visit such a teacher and discuss progress in work in the college and changing attitudes towards future plans for jobs or courses in colleges, etc.

At the present, the school does not take enough interest in one's future career. One receives one's U.C.C.A. Form, fills it in, and that is it. Compulsory or semi-compulsory interviews for discussion personally, of the job opportunities etc., are not provided, and should be.

Given the importance that students clearly attach to an individual approach, the system of tutor-counsellors and guidance staff operated by an increasing number of upper-secondary schools and colleges is a welcome development. But the success of such a system depends to a great extent on the knowledge and experience of the staff concerned and the degree to which they co-ordinate their efforts.

Particular problems therefore face the staff of sixth form colleges and other institutions to which students come at the age of 16-plus. In these cases a considerable amount of time and effort is needed to build up a detailed picture of individual students' interests, aptitudes, aspirations etc., for one has no lower-secondary experience to rely on. This problem can be — and in some areas of the country is — alleviated by the transfer of detailed records from secondary school to the upper-secondary institution. Yet there is a body of opinion which strongly condemns this practice on the grounds that students should embark on upper-secondary education with a 'clean slate' and should not gain or lose as a result of their earlier performance. Besides, the consideration is not confined to previous behaviour and scholastic performance. The need for a 'fresh start' includes an opportunity to *change* interests and courses. In any case, the upper-secondary content of many courses differs from that in the lower school, performance in which may be a poor predictor of performance beyond 16. These *are* persuasive arguments. On balance it seems preferable to give upper-secondary guidance staff the time and facilities needed to get to know individual students.

Clearly students' teachers have an advantage in this respect. But should they also act as counsellors and guidance staff? We have already discussed some of the pros and cons. Many anxieties and personal problems can be dealt with perfectly adequately by sympathetic, perceptive and sensitive teachers given the necessary time and facilities. But at the level of more serious family, sexual or emotional difficulties, there is a strong argument in favour of providing trained counsellors who do not teach the students concerned, and whose 'approachability' stems from having clear links with the world outside school or college.

A Dual System for Counselling and Guidance: The Need Expressed

Both forms of counselling are therefore desirable and necessary. So a welcome development would be the introduction of a *dual* system in schools and colleges. Such a system would enable students to consult a personal tutor, whom they already knew, about day-to-day problems. But those with more serious and intimate difficulties could choose to approach a trained counsellor if they felt that they needed more 'objective' and 'anonymous' help, perhaps involving external agencies. Trained counsellors could serve more than one school or college (although two would probably be a workable maximum number). They should be available both inside and outside normal school or college hours; and if possible counsellors should be involved in the daily life of the school or college, in a *non-teaching* capacity. This last point is a particularly important one.

It is vital for counsellors to be familiar with the characteristics of the school or college in which they work. Otherwise they run the risk of being regarded by staff and students as *too* remote. Yet it seems equally vital that they should not become indentified with the teaching staff. One way of striking a balance would be for counsellors to take part in mainly non-teaching activities, although this is not to deny that *previous* teaching experience would be an asset.

The dual system proposed has a number of advantages. Perhaps chief among them are that students would be able to choose whom they consult according to their needs, and that tutor-counsellors would be freed from some of their current anxieties about the limits of their function.

The question of *resources* must also be considered. In the present economic climate it would be irresponsible to advocate measures involving increased expenditure without first carefully weighing up the pros and cons. We have referred to the problems of scarce resources, both monetary and manpower. Yet the arguments in favour of providing trained counsellors are hard to ignore. As the Schools Council has pointed out, it would be false economy to recruit counsellors from the ranks of teachers, or to insist that these two roles be combined for 'Every new counsellor will be a part-time teacher lost, not gained' (op. cit.). Some redistribution of resources would clearly be necessary, as recent proposals for financing non-teaching services permit (e.g., for librarian/study advisors). Since in other areas of educational expenditure priorities are being re-thought, why not for counselling? To quote the Schools Council once more — can we afford *not* to provide an adequate counselling service in our schools and colleges?

Let us now turn from counselling on personal problems to the provision of careers guidance and educational guidance. We have already emphasised that many young people prefer an individual approach and stress the importance of being able to obtain information and advice from someone who knows them — their interests, aptitudes, abilities and aspirations — personally. But at the same time students stressed the need for *careers guidance* staff to be fully in touch with the whole range of employment and educational opportunities. The following student comment is typical of many:

> This school requires someone, not necessarily working here, who is fully aware of university and employment opportunities. But he, or she, must be concerned with this, and this alone. The existing system here where the job of careers master seems to be reluctantly taken on by a teacher who for some reason has a less full timetable than others is absolutely useless. (*Post-Compulsory Education I*, op. cit., 355 ff).

Other students felt that 'practical help from persons in the type of job or profession you are considering' would be valuable, and indeed we have already seen that 10% of all students in England who took part in our own research requested talks by people in various occupations.

So here we have the crux of the problem. Those who are closest to the students have little — if any — first-hand knowledge of many employment and external educational opportunities. Those who *do* — such as workers in various jobs and advisory fields, and careers officers — have little or no contact with post-compulsory students; they have, therefore, no real knowledge of the personal crises they may face.

Towards a Dual System of Counselling and Guidance: Practical Moves

How can the different competences and approaches be combined or harmonised in practice? The alternatives are:

a. To familiarise guidance teachers with as wide a range of educational and employment opportunities as possible.
b. To enable careers officers and workers in various occupations to play a larger part in the guidance process.
c. To create a 'new breed of animal' — a new concept of careers and educational guidance in schools and colleges involving a new type of guidance personnel.

Let us consider the first of these alternatives. The problem of familiarising teachers with the outside employment world (educational opportunities present fewer difficulties) has been under discussion for a number of years. In 1966 the Schools Council brought out a Working Paper on this subject.* The principal aims of the 'introduction to industry' scheme it recommended were to:

a. 'give teachers insight into the experiences of young people entering working life';

---

*Schools Council Working Paper 7, *Closer Links Between Teachers and Industry and Commerce* (HMSO, 1966).

b. 'provide teachers with a better appreciation of the educational and other standards employers expect their young entrants to attain'; and

c. 'bring about a greater understanding between employers and teachers'.

By 1972 some 2000 teachers from over fifty local education authorities in Britain had taken part in the scheme, organised in collaboration with the Confederation of British Industry and with local industry and commerce. The scheme has generally been regarded as valuable by all concerned. It should be pointed out that the scheme is intended for *all* teachers, not specially those with careers guidance responsibilities. Even if such a scheme could be extended to meet the particular needs of careers teachers, it is doubtful whether those needs would effectively be met. The range of employment opportunities that would need to be covered would pose almost insuperable problems of time and other resources.

The second alternative is to enable careers officers and workers in various occupations to play a larger part in the guidance process.

As we have seen, careers officers are already hard-pressed, and it is difficult to see how they can take on a very much greater role than they have now, given the present structure of the careers service.

One possibility would be to second careers officers to individual schools and colleges for a period of time, during which they would be available to deal with students' questions and problems. It should be stressed that their role would be a purely advisory one, and that careers officers would in no way be responsible for job placement. The secondment could be on a full-time or a part-time basis, and could cover more than one institution.

This suggestion poses obvious problems. While it would have the strong advantage of bringing careers officers and students into much closer contact, it would — unless recruitment could be increased — aggravate existing staff shortages in the careers service. The position of the careers officer in a school or college could possibly be a difficult one for the teaching staff to accept — particularly those with guidance responsibilities. Competition and conflict rather than co-operation might follow, and this would obviously be highly undesirable.

The more frequent use of workers in a variety of occupations is a more feasible proposition. They could be invited into schools and colleges to talk about their field of employment and to answer students' questions (as now, but on a much bigger and better co-ordinated scale). Their contribution may obviously be a very subjective one; yet it provides students with the first-hand information 'straight from the horse's mouth' which so many young adults say they would welcome, but do not get. Clearly, care has to be taken to ensure that such encounters do not constitute informal recruitment drives on the part of employers. The main aim of any such scheme is to help fill the gap in students' direct contacts with people who have first-hand knowledge and experience of particular fields of employment. It need not in any way resemble the present often dreary lectures by representatives of the Civil Service, the Armed Forces, and so on.

The third alternative would be to create a 'new breed of animal, a new type of advisor'.

The question of trained specialist careers and educational advisors — other than careers officers — was raised in our research report.* Our recommendations were very similar to

---

Post-Compulsory Education I: A New Analysis in Western Europe

those of the DES Inspectorate in their 1973 report on *Careers Education in Secondary Schools,* which was published soon after our report was completed.

We suggested then, and again recommend here, that — as in the case of personal counselling — there should be a *dual* system of careers and educational guidance, provided by teacher-tutors on the one hand and specialist advisors on the other. These would work in close co-operation.

The school or college tutors would possess valuable knowledge of individual students' interests, aptitudes, attainments and aspirations, obtained in the course of continuous personal contact with the young adults concerned. On the basis of the tutors' personal knowledge, the specialist advisors would have the task of providing individual students with suitable information and guidance.

The specialist advisors would need to possess a wide-ranging, accurate and up-to-date picture of opportunities and the ability to relate these to young people's interests, aspirations and attainments. This 'new breed' would be attached to a school or college, and would work from it. They would be full-time workers, with no teaching duties but preferably some teaching experience. They would be specially trained to carry out the tasks of advising individual students, maintaining liaison with teachers, tutors and employers, and keeping abreast of new developments.

So for both personal counselling and careers and educational guidance we recommend a *two-tier system.* At the first level in both cases are the teacher-tutors who possess valuable knowledge of individual students, built up through

---

(1974), 376 ff. The whole of Chapter 18 gives a detailed survey of counselling and guidance needs and trends in England and other Western European countries.

continuous personal contact with the young people concerned. Tutors would be responsible for providing the trained counsellors and specialist advisers who operate at the second level with detailed information on individual students. (In the case of personal counselling, of course, the tutors would be responsible for dealing with day-to-day problems and anxieties.) Obviously, people working at these two levels would need to co-operate closely and continuously with each other.

RECOMMENDATIONS FOR CURRICULUM: PERSPECTIVES FOR TEACHERS AND ORGANIZERS

In considering the day-to-day process of adapting curricula and contacts, it is taken for granted that everything will hinge on those changes of perception and relationship which this book and its predecessor have shown to be necessary. Though references are made generally to 'schools' and 'colleges', for convenience, the focus is on evolving provision expressly intended for young adult students in the post-compulsory phase of education.

The recommendations which follow are not ideal; yet they are practicable (if not already proven), and they do show guidelines appropriate to British or similar circumstances. They are considered under 5 main heads: academic studies; vocational/technical courses; 'general education' for non-specialists; combined studies; and extra-curricular activities.

Local applicability to Britain may make some of the language used seem rather 'schooly' and perhaps old-fashioned elsewhere; but the recommendations made in this section should be seen as no more than a point of departure on a journey of continuous re-orientation. In

Britain and some other countries that departure has already been made by pioneers; but a start on re-orientation is urgent if it has not already been made. Therefore the risk of over-simplification is accepted in spelling out some necessities. These will seem obvious to the already enterprising, although they manifestly shocked many school and college authorities encountered during our research.

First, however, two pivotal principles for action:

a. *Equality of opportunity for study*

The first requisite is to provide equivalent opportunities for study for all 16+ students. In England this will be a more complex process than in most other European countries, where a high degree of centralisation often makes it possible to insist on changes across the whole country. Wide differences in the kind of provision offered make some student 'choices' an accident of geography rather than a real choice. 'Equivalent', of course, does not mean 'identical', but a range of choices equally open to all those eager to take them up and showing ability to do so.

b. *'Provisional' choice of study and/or training*

In upper-secondary education learning requirements are different from those in lower-secondary education. Although subjects may have the same name in upper- and lower-secondary education the content and kind of study involved may be very different. Student motivation, achievement and aspirations are not constant but subject to change for personal, social, academic, and career reasons. Therefore it seems reasonable to regard curricular choices as provisional for at least the first stage of post-compulsory education. That provisional character applies both to choice of studies and to their possible usefulness for admission to further study or a career. That entails close co-operation between the guidance/counselling agencies and those responsible for curriculum.

Academic Courses of Study

It is difficult to make specific suggestions about academic curricular reform in England and Wales while the 3 A-Level specialist subject pattern for *examinations* in the General Certificate of Education has such a stranglehold on *curriculum.* Recommendations are made therefore according to two possible situations with regard to examinations:

i. assuming the worst, i.e. that the A-Level examination remains unchanged;
ii. assuming that the A-Level examination will be changed or replaced.

i. If A-Level is to remain in its present form, then it is unreasonable that so many students, especially those not intending or likely to proceed to traditional kinds of higher education, are forced by customary timetables to follow a rigidly specialist 3-subject pattern for most of their studies. Often these rigid groupings are the result of enforced choices made several years earlier. Many schools and colleges either through tradition or inertia, or through pressure from the universities and their joint examination boards, maintain this pattern. They could (as our evidence showed):

a. offer a wider choice of subjects at this level;
b. choose or devise modern variant syllabuses permitted *within* the subjects selected for A-Level (e.g. really modern European history, or the socio-economic geography of important regions);
c. be more flexible in allowing students to *start* subjects

for A-Level;

d. allow 'academic' A-Levels to be combined with technical, commercial, practical or lower-level studies;

e. take advantage of (or develop) new examining modes (e.g. Mode III) which permit more active participation by teachers in the evaluation process;

f. provide a well thought out and vigorous complementary programme of general studies.

(However, as such recommendations have been *constantly urged* (and practicable) for many years *to very little effect,* it seems more hopeful to consider a different pattern of academic studies altogether.)

ii. Any alternative pattern of academic studies would have to fulfil certain requirements: universities would have to be satisfied that candidates were of a certain standard; students would have to be satisfied that there was sufficient choice and that the courses were relevant to them personally; teachers would have to feel that they could exercise choice and develop their particular subject strengths; and the system as a whole would have to be educationally justifiable. In particular it would be important that any pattern of academic studies should not be conceived *only* as a university entrance qualification, since even university and other higher education authorities recognise the unwisdom of doing so.

Other European systems often show a situation which is the obverse of the English. Reformers have tended to *reduce* the large number of subjects studied and to allow more emphasis on some subjects, thus permitting a degree of specialisation within a still 'general' education. However, two faults persist: there has not always been an accompanying reform of teaching methods; and the subjects for a particular 'line' or grouped course are nearly always presented *en bloc,* leading to restriction of student choice and inflexibility in curricular readjustment.

For England at present the best examination system for students with clear academic intentions would seem to be a variation on the International Baccalaureate model. In this, students study six subjects, three at a Higher Level, three at a Subsidiary Level, together with the equivalent of one afternoon a week devoted to an 'aesthetic' activity, plus a compulsory course on the theory of knowledge which is designed to integrate the kinds of thinking used in other studies. The distribution of Higher and Subsidiary Levels in the International Baccalaureate means that every examination candidate includes in his pattern of studies: a first and second language, mathematics, an experimental science, a human science, and a sixth subject at free choice. Six subjects (plus marks for the theory of knowledge and assessment of the creative, aesthetic element) are offered for university entrance or equivalent qualification; but subjects may also be taken individually.

English teachers may jib at the idea of six examinable subjects; but the Schools Council Working Party Paper No. 45 suggests other variations. A very similar disposition of studies was recommended in 1963 by the conference of European teachers supported by the Council of Europe. In any case the general shift of emphasis in favour of breadth and choice remains valid for reasons given at several points throughout this book. Such a system offers considerable scope for variety, flexibility and varying degrees of commitment to academic study.

More specifically, the *advantages* of such a system can be listed as follows:

a. There are no fixed 'lines' or compulsorily grouped courses as in some continental systems.

b. A school or college can build on its particular strengths and still offer a widely acceptable university entrance qualification to those students who want it (of equivalent value to qualifications offered by other schools and colleges, and already *preferred* by many university admissions officers).

c. The syllabuses for the various subjects are broad enough to allow great variety of treatment and illustrative topics.

d. There is an attempt at integration through the theory of knowledge paper.

e. The system of assessment is more comprehensive than A-Level assessment procedures.

f. The possibility of specialising for examination purposes in a few subjects from the range offered gives a flexibility of choice to students who wish to combine pre-university academic studies with, for example, the non-examination studies which all students follow, or specifically vocational courses.

g. The system avoids the proliferation of subjects at various levels which is to be found in some sixth-form institutions, and which is expensive in terms of staff time and effort.

The research reported in our earlier book showed that one sixth-form college, for example, ran thirteen separate mathematics courses, and offered many subjects for which the number of student takers was very small. A smaller range of subjects, treated with much greater sensitivity, allowing many permutations of choice (between subjects and within the subjects themselves) would be more viable and more economical; yet it would also be far more open to student diversity, to interdisciplinary combinations of interest, and to modernisation than are most traditional arrangements.

The *disadvantages* of such a system for present

consideration are as follows:

    a. The examination system would be more expensive than that used for A-Level. (However, if O-Level were abandoned, or replaced by a simpler, common form of examining at 16+, that would release more money to be spent on upper-secondary examinations.)

    b. The International Baccalaureate was designed for the 'academic' pupil. It is not yet clear whether its courses (or something similar) could be adapted to other types of students; e.g. those who, at present, are taking part in the experimental preparation for the Certificate of Extended Education in one of the forms considered in the Schools Council Working Party Paper No. 45.

    c. Such a system could leave the present organisation of subject departments in schools and colleges unchanged. It will be argued later in this section that this organisation could be radically changed to encourage more teamwork, with benefit to students — and to staff.

Vocational/Technical Courses

It is clear from what has been said throughout this book, and from such publications as the *Janne-Géminard Report* (1973), that commitment to a particular type of vocational education should be delayed or made provisional because of continuing changes in the occupational structure.

However, certain guidelines can be suggested:

    i. Vocationally oriented courses should contain practical experience 'on the job' (as already happens in sandwich courses, though less often in the 16-20 range) not just to give specific training, which may become outdated, but to illustrate experientially the range and nature of working and learning relationships, and to show what it is like to work in an organisation other than an 'educational' one.

ii. As with 'academic' studies, vocational studies should be flexible enough to allow students freedom of choice within a range; and it should be easier than now to combine academic and vocational studies.

iii. Vocational studies should not be limited to job-related tasks, since many 'human studies' are of vocational as well as personal relevance. Most workers, for example, will be members of trade unions; all will have the right to vote; many service industry jobs depend on linguistic and social skills as much as on specific technical competences; and many workers (academic or otherwise) may well have more leisure time. It would be foolhardy to neglect skills and perceptions necessary for these aspects of adult life.

iv. As with 'academic' studies, there should be an integrative element. In many vocational/technical courses this aspect is rather unsatisfactory. Many students do not see the relevance to them of integrative studies, which are often taught 'from outside' or as 'an extra' by people from 'servicing' departments, e.g. the Liberal or General Studies Departments in Colleges of Further Education. It is argued that a reorganisation of staff — and still more a change of internal attitude and personal relationships — could help solve this problem.

'General Education' Courses for non-Specialists

It must be admitted that this label has been used for want of better. Within the English system there are a growing number of students over 16 who are following non-examination courses, or courses where examination passes will be minimal. Some schools and colleges try to devise special courses for them; others distribute these students between various O-Level and technical groups. Such students are likely to come off worst of all those being educated at this level, since they are not always improving either their academic or career chances.

This student group are therefore in need of special consideration. Curricular plans for them need to be made in close consultation with guidance and counselling staff. Some students might be better advised to start work and come back into education at a later date; some need to be advised against making choices which probably will not help them fulfil eventual career aspirations; some are unready to make any sort of specific or even provisional decision about their future, but may be encouraged to try a range of studies or work experience schemes. In no case should such students be dismissed as an unwelcome, ill-defined category but helped through a programme of study and guidance to develop and come to a realistic decision about their future. This recommendation again raises questions of staff organisation, and introduces consideration of the development of consortia to make full use of institutions, facilities, and personal contacts.

Combined Studies in New Fields of Special Interest

It has been pointed out that division into rigid 'lines' is not desirable. Some students are happy with an academic education, some with a more technical bias, but it should be possible for students to combine these interests. Some universities now offer combined degrees (e.g. Engineering and Modern Languages, European Studies, or Environmental Studies) which combine arts, sciences and social sciences; so it should be still more possible for those enrolled in post-compulsory education to follow 'combined' courses of study. Again this raises questions for staff organisation, study patterns, and the nature of co-operation between different institutions or departments. There are also questions of possible follow-up in later courses of study, in career possibilities, and in external supplementation (e.g. by broadcasting and other supporting services).

Extra-Curricular Activities

These, increasingly, are becoming 'curricular'; i.e. they are recognised as having intrinsic educational worth, and thus claim time within the formal programme of most schools and colleges. That is far less true of vocational institutions, and hardly true at all of the continent. Often the existence of effective extra-curricular activities has depended on the enthusiasm or expertise of teachers or students who have given up their time. More should be done to encourage the development of extra-curricular activities through allocation of special responsibility allowances and by specific training of teachers or other supporting personnel. Such 'training' is not so much teacher-training as training for educating young adults in social development, and becoming an *animateur* of young adults' increasingly autonomous processes of self-development — especially in the perspective of 'recurrent education' of both specific and general kinds.

The above recommendations for the 'overt' or 'provided' curriculum take into account the need expressed (by students and staff) for such elements as: personal choice; a range of interests; and in particular the opportunity to study the social sciences, together with some integrated or interdisciplinary study. However, such recommendations are of little avail without accompanying changes in the way in which curricular elements are taught, or rather *learnt.* After all, one can make permutations of subjects *ad infinitum,* yet do nothing to ensure that students are educated in the essential processes: acquiring knowledge; exercising the skills of learning; using what is learned to personal, social and practical benefit; becoming sensitised to human relationships; and developing an adult commitment to the responsibilities of civilisation. Given even the best of 'provided' curricula, students may learn very different curricular 'messages'. Therefore we now consider the students' curricular experience.

THE CURRICULUM – AS EXPERIENCED BY STUDENTS

The following recommendations are couched in terms of teaching/learning relationships as students experience them, and consider the *processes* of learning. Education is as much a social as an intellectual activity. Whereas it is relatively easy to categorise areas of knowledge for the purposes of making up a 'traditional-style' curriculum, it is less easy to ensure the development of personal skills and commitment during the teaching of that curriculum. For this reason this section emphasises the 'curricular experience' of the learner.

The most important elements seem to be:

i.   Analysis of the basic concepts and factual elements of a 'subject' or area of knowledge, and of the ways in which these are related. Various Schools Council projects have claimed to do this, particularly in interdisciplinary areas of interest; but students are seldom given enough help in determining concepts and criteria.*

---

*For a full treatment of the point see Douglas Holly's *Beyond Curriculum* (1974).

ii. Mitigation — perhaps abandonment where possible — of the custom of 'class' teaching. The idea of students covering an identical programme, at an identical pace, in competition with each other to reach the highest marks in a situation where contact is between teacher and students (not between student and student, or between student and the topic studied) should be done away with. Co-operative working groups which sometimes meet as a class, sometimes engage in individual work, and sometimes work in small groups, should largely replace traditional classes.

iii. The development of personal learning skills. That implies a change of role for the teacher. Instead of being essentially a dispenser of knowledge he becomes a guide, a motivator, a diagnostician, a leader, a manager of a learning environment.

iv. The development of aids to learning. Some time ago this item might have been called 'audio-visual aids' or 'technical aids'. Audio-visual techniques imperfectly used or adapted can merely reproduce (expensively) traditional lessons in a way which causes a student to learn on his own what he previously might have learnt in a class. But judicious use of audio-visual techniques and other resources (e.g. of modern information retrieval) allows students to go at their own pace, or catch up what they may have missed elsewhere. Specially developed case-studies, simulations or 'games' which can be cheaply reproduced for a specific course may be more useful than mass-produced teaching materials which may have a limited life.

v. Student participation in planning the development of learning. Usually students follow a course laid down for them by teachers or others, and their performance is evaluated impersonally at the end of the year. More frequently discussion with a student of his own strengths, weaknesses and needs should allow teachers to counsel him throughout an individual work programme developed from work done with a group or directly feeding into it.

vi. The development of co-operative learning. Too often students are encouraged to be in competition with each other. Instead they should be encouraged to contribute to and use the expertise and skills of the groups.

vii. Development of the ability to use knowledge and re-order it to plan alternative futures. Education at this level is especially concerned with values. The traditional role of the teacher has been to 'hand on' those values which have seemed most worthwhile, or at best to 'initiate' students into accepting a perennial system of priorities. There is now more need to plan for an uncertain future. That involves giving more attention and time to the social sciences, to an exploration of the acquisition and development of values. Although this activity might have been listed as an 'extra' within the formal curriculum, it is really concerned with the experiential development of *self*-knowledge and a *personal testing out* of assumptions and values. This has implications not only for the teaching/learning situation but for the participation of students in the internal organisation of their school or college.*

---

*For a full treatment of this point see A. Toffler (ed.), *Learning for Tomorrow: The Role of the Future in Education* (1974). It is also important to consider in this connection some American and continental evidence, including some reported in our earlier book.

viii. Opportunity for all-round personal development through extra-curricular activities and other responsibilities, including participation in the direction of learning. The management of student clubs and equipment is important; but much more so is membership of college committees and — where possible — of the Board of Governors.

PHASING, TIMING AND DEGREES OF COMMITMENT

Too often courses or subjects at the 16-20 level have been thought of as necessarily having a fixed duration; students have either been in full-time study or on day-release. There have been day classes and evening classes with little cross-over between the two. Given the development of more institutions catering for the 16-plus group, and given the growing feeling that post-compulsory education is a first stage in adult education, the following recommendations should be taken into account:

i. Adults should be allowed back into post-compulsory education at an upper-secondary level if that is in their best interests.
ii. More experiments with sandwich courses should be carried out.
iii. Students should be allowed varying degrees of commitment to study, and various patterns of time-allocation (e.g. continuous full-time education, or full-time over short periods, or evenings only, or part-time). In each case, appropriate support systems must be available. (There are many precedents in many countries — not necessarily costing more than traditional

means of education.)

iv. Despite the tendency in some countries to build big community campuses, small 'half-way houses' should be available outside large organisations for people who feel that they cannot become part of the 'educational establishment' or feel at home in an enormous system.

INTERNAL ORGANISATION OF SCHOOLS AND COLLEGES

The acceptance of the recommendations listed above implies for many teachers an acceptance of a new set of priorities: the need for self-realisation and self-education on the part of students; acceptance of a pluralist system of values; and commitment to establishing more adult staff/student relationships in schools or colleges for the over-16s. What are the implications for the internal organisation of schools and colleges? Most of the remarks which follow deal expressly with the British situation — often with reference to schools or colleges still not fully alerted to the educational needs of normal young adults, or even to the rapid changes overtaking the world of learning as these affect supposedly 'traditional' students and careers.

In Britain, unfortunately, reorganisation of the internal management of an establishment even for young adults is still often thought of mainly in terms of relaxing rules about clothing, smoking, hair-styles, etc. While many more school/college authorities recognise that a more reasonable, adult atmosphere should be encouraged, so far there have been few radical proposals as to how staff organisation itself might best be re-arranged to meet a new set of values and objectives.

The usual British staffing arrangement is to have a head or

principal, with one or more deputies, and then a series of subject departments. Pastoral arrangements are sometimes completely separate, sometimes interwoven with subject responsibilities. Some schools and colleges have a 'cabinet' to include heads of departments, to discuss curricular policy. The role of the sixth-form subject teacher in such circumstances is akin to that of a British university lecturer gathering his disciples around him, with a certain amount of discussion and individual study. Some experiments have been made with team teaching, but not many. It must be admitted that much teaching at this level is more formal than has been described. (On the continent it is nearly always extremely formal.)

Our own and others' research findings showed a great gap in perception between students and teachers about what was desirable and feasible at this level. The learning needs strongly expressed by students were:

a. to learn through satisfactory personal relationships;
b. to perceive the material learned as relevant to them personally; and
c. to see how all learning fits together.

It would be an interesting innovation to organise most teachers in post-compulsory education not under subject divisions as at present but into teams with corporate responsibility for particular groups of students. This kind of syndicate arrangement is already familiar in various kinds of staff-training establishments in Britain and some famous American universities. It is also a well-tried principle in adult education.

The extension of such a pattern to post-compulsory education would avoid the fragmentation which so many students perceive. What does it involve in practical terms?

Teachers would have to see themselves as extended, rather than limited, professionals; they would have less autonomy in their own immediate environment but more power to weld a course together. The process of discussing programmes, allocating time, and integrating with other subjects and teachers needs not just a good 'academic' and a good learner but a good team-leader, since it involves 'managerial' skills in development. If teachers want to develop in their students personal learning skills, co-operation, and other desiderata for young adults' learning, then they cannot avoid putting these into operation themselves.

The development of perceptions and skills necessary for corporate effort is already seen in some courses offered by colleges of education. In-service training programmes offer much more promise, however. Manifestly, too, it will be necessary to make full use of the possibilities of non-teaching or partly teaching personnel, such as librarians and 'learning resources' officers, as well as teachers in the familiar sense. But all such staff will need sensitising to the post-compulsory students' special needs, just as teachers do.

IMPLICATIONS FOR PRE- AND IN-SERVICE TRAINING OF TEACHERS

In earlier chapters we have at several points discussed the initial preparation and training of teachers for the 16-20 age-range. We have pointed to the need to make sure that they understand the newness of their task in general, and are ready for the particular responsibilities of teaching young adults today — especially in experimental institutions and relationships. One usual weakness of both preparatory and in-service courses is lack of integration between education theory, teaching/learning practice, and the wider sensitivity now required. Many teacher-training courses, like schools, are still subject-oriented rather than task- or group-oriented. We therefore draw attention to the need to make use of the colleges' and schools' own evolutionary processes as an essential part of teacher-*training* in connection with this age-group, and not only for the general reasons given in the James Report and similar recommendations.

When discussing students' education we emphasised the need for external contacts and on-the-job realism. Our suggestions for teacher education and especially training reflect a similar concern. The important difference here, of course, is that teachers' on-the-job learning is within the schools and colleges. Much more *training* can and should be undertaken there, and also some kinds of learning about educating young adults, without prejudice to what must be learned outside.

Team-building, co-operation, joint decisions about what is best done, sharing out resources – in short, learning how to *manage* to achieve objectives within specific restraints in a given context – are matters for *internal* and experiential learning, and therefore should be developed as far as possible in the real-life circumstances of schools and colleges. Close contact with all external agencies of information and support is taken for granted.

It has several times been emphasised that teachers themselves must participate as team members in any process of innovation or reorientation, if that is to have real prospects of success. (One by-product of our method of investigation was to show in actual practice the feasibility of that partnership.) Young adult students should be involved too. This requirement logically extends not only to the planning and mapping-out of their own course work but also to active participation in the implementation and management of innovation, and its evaluation.

Short in-service courses for teachers often preach to the converted, or at least to the willing. In any case they are intermittent, and course members are still often faced with an intractable task when they return to schools and colleges. Consultants in education management (in which there is a growing interest) can be brought in to help schools and colleges with the actual processes involved in managing a particular innovation. Research and development activities as well as tailor-made courses based outside school can usefully re-develop 'subject areas' and professional subjects for new-style presentation; and the supply of texts, manuals and other supporting resources (including broadcasts) can gradually replace much less appropriate materials.

There is much need for development and reinforcement of serving teachers. Considerable evidence suggests that any benefit derived from good initial training quickly wears off in an unfavourable environment. Therefore it might well be advisable to rely far less on initial teacher *training,* and to use far more extensively the staff and resources of colleges, polytechnics and universities in concert with recurrent in-service training or re-orientation, particularly in helping younger teachers through their first years in the profession. That observation applies especially at a time when teachers' closeness to young adults (actual or potential) is put at risk because of pressure to fit into established practice and institutional forms. Those external contacts with the world of learning and research extend the horizon beyond the school and its immediate concerns, thus helping to introduce questions of wider relevance.

CONCLUDING REMARKS ON CURRICULAR REORIENTATION

To conclude this curricular part of our recommendations, we return to the remarks made in its introductory paragraphs. No piece of detailed comment or advice can be appropriate by itself, since each suggestion takes real meaning only from the context of reorientation in post-compulsory education as a whole. That in its turn forms part of exceedingly rapid evolution in education generally; yet in some ways post-compulsory education by the very newness characterising it seems central to the reorientation, if not transformation, of many learning relationships throughout life. All educational relationships are shifting fast: in learning new knowledge; using and developing that knowledge in unfamiliar circumstances; coping with practical problems of continuous decision; and in simply learning how to live and learn effectively together. But the young adults in post-compulsory education − by their very position − are the frontiersmen and pioneers of much new learning.

Therefore it cannot be too strongly stressed that the authors by no means tie their recommendations to present institutions either in school/college systems or in the socio-economic system of any country. Indeed many parts of public life, and many information and learning systems outside the official educational provision, are far better evolved to suit the needs of today's 'communications society' than the majority of scholastic institutions.

Among the latter, a significant minority of higher education institutions are already giving the lead by a remarkable conceptual turnabout; they are restructuring course-work and outside contacts, re-grouping and re-phasing studies, and gradually adopting a different attitude to the recognition and development of scholarship and skills of every kind. Accordingly, whatever may be decided in any school, college, course or teaching/learning contact must be seen as an integral part of that same process of rebuilding the world of learning.

OUR FINAL RECOMMENDATION

An enormous amount of goodwill and practical experience in post-compulsory education has been built up in Britain during the past few decades. The auguries are good for a happy solution of many problems in that field. In fact, British experiments — and still more the openness of British education to experimentation — have won the admiration of innovators across the world.

But innovation is one thing; sustaining and developing innovation are quite different. Drawing systematically on innovation for a developing *policy* rich in pragmatic insights marks yet a further stage. Research findings accumulate, too, but lie scattered around. Despite the gatherings of administrators, principals, and even Ministers, the risk is that this growing body of evidence and experience may remain little more than a 'climate of opinion' or a 'state of readiness'.

Readiness for what? Undoubtedly readiness for *a national policy on post-compulsory education*. To gather up, consider, and draw policy recommendations from all available evidence, a permanent organisation of services and advice for post-compulsory education seems imperative. As a matter of urgency we recommend that a National Commission be set up now to consider all the evidence, and to make policy recommendations for the immediate future.

APPENDIX 1

A Model for the Analysis of 'Newness' (Especially in Education, 16-20)

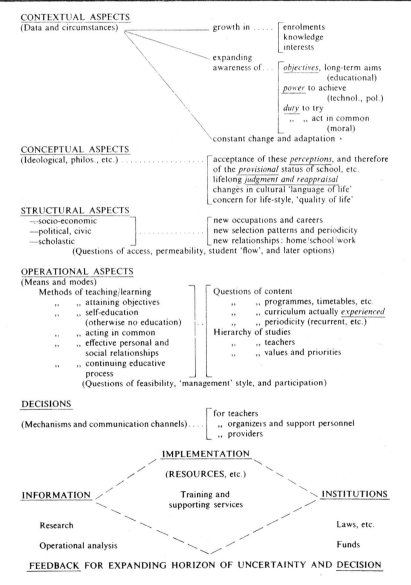

Reproduced by permission from *Comparative Education*, Vol. 11, No. 1 (1975).

APPENDIX 2

A Methodological Note

An outline of our research approach and some of its practical problems are presented in the Introduction. Many more details, with a critique of our method and a cautionary note on international comparisons, are available in chapters 1-3 of *Post-Compulsory Education I: A New Analysis in Western Europe.*

Enthusiasts for methodology will notice that our earlier research study preserved the three-stage analysis recommended elsewhere for comparative studies. It set out from a careful recognition of the context to make distinctions between the conceptual, structural, and operational aspects of a 'real' problem recognised as such by the participants in the educational system, and then moved on to a study of feasible decisions and possible programmes.

Before ever the Comparative Research Unit's investigations began, however, the team satisfied Sir Karl Popper's 'hypothetical-deductive' requirements by the detailed statement of intent for the project which was submitted to the Social Science Research Council, and by the subsidiary proposals and operational hypotheses which won the co-operation of researchers and Ministries in five countries. With their help, and with feedback from the field (Popper's 'plastic controls with feedback'), the instruments and forms of analysis or interpretation used were continually shaped for the precise purpose of obtaining the 'inside view' and evaluating it with as much ground 'participation' as possible. In other words, research method evolved as the research problem evolved under investigation.

Two supporting quotations from Professor Popper seem appropriate:

> When we speak of a problem, we do so almost always from hindsight. A man who works on a problem can seldom say clearly what his problem is (unless he has found a solution); and even if he can explain his problem, he may mistake it. (*Of Clouds and Clocks* (1966), 26).

> The more fruitful debates on method are always inspired by certain practical problems which face the research worker; and nearly all debates on method which are not so inspired are characterised by that atmosphere of futile subtlety which has brought methodology into disrepute with the practical research worker'. (*Poverty of Historicism* (1957), 57).

We therefore feel that our initial analysis of problems in real-life post-compulsory education, our programming and adaptation of empirical fieldwork, and our subsequent incorporation of feedback from evolving experiments, have added three elements of freshness to comparative studies of education.

INDEX